THE
TEST & COUNTY
CRICKET BOARD
GUIDE TO
BETTER
CRICKET

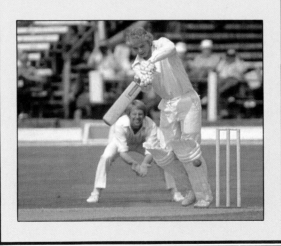

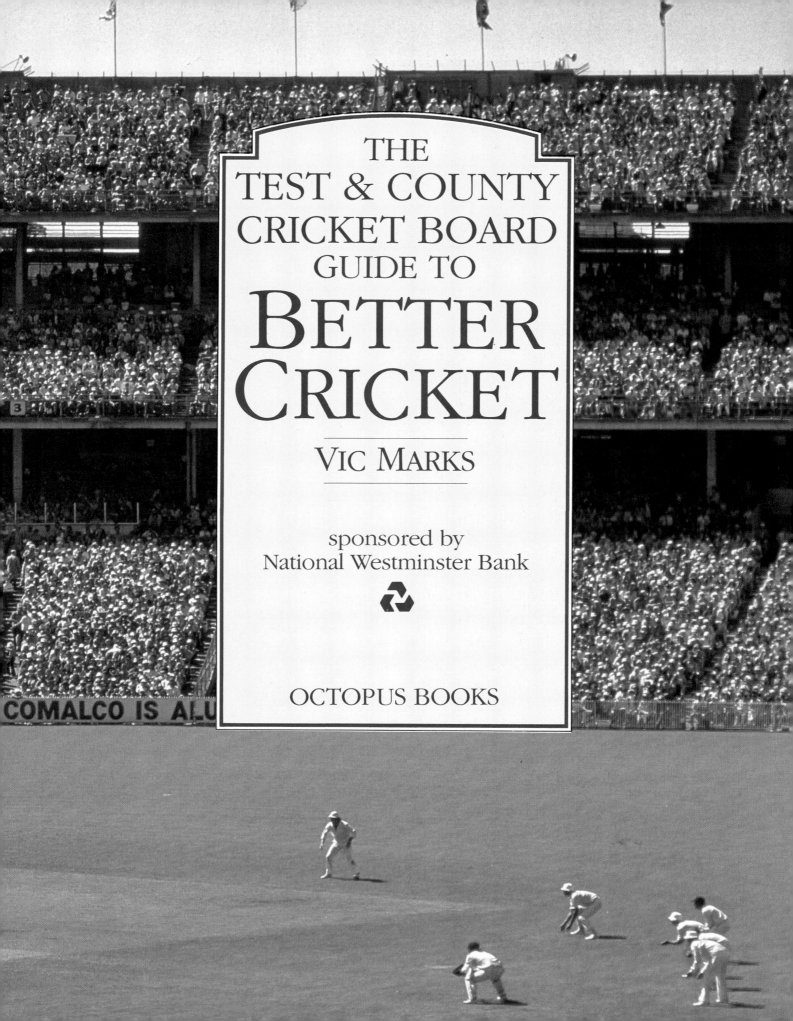

THE
TEST & COUNTY
CRICKET BOARD
GUIDE TO
BETTER
CRICKET

VIC MARKS

sponsored by
National Westminster Bank

OCTOPUS BOOKS

First published in 1987 by
Octopus Books Limited
59 Grosvenor Street
London W1

ISBN 0−7064−3047−6

Editor: Tessa Rose

Copy-editor: Diana Vowles

Designer: Bob Gordon

Illustrations: John Raynes

Motifs: Andrew Farmer

Statistics: Peter Arnold

Production: Peter Thompson/Audrey Johnston

Typeset by MS Filmsetting Limited, Frome, Somerset
Colour origination by Mandarin, Hong Kong
Printed and bound in Spain by Graficromo, Cordoba

Note: The figures given in the career profiles are correct
to the end of the 1986/7 season.

Captions
Half-title: David Gower
Title: Lillee bowls to Knott, Centenary Test, Melbourne, 1977

CONTENTS

FOREWORD

By the Chairman of the National Westminster Bank PLC

I am delighted with the initiative taken by the Test & County Cricket Board to produce this book which National Westminster Bank has sponsored.

Written by Vic Marks (Oxford University, Somerset & England) with the technical assistance of Keith Andrew (Northamptonshire & England), Chief Executive of the National Cricket Association, I am sure that this publication will be lovingly and inquisitively referred to by enthusiasts of all ages and abilities for many years to come.

The National Cricket Association's video and coaching films, which were also sponsored by National Westminster Bank, provide any school teacher or club coach with a formidable armoury. This book will further assist an appreciation of the finer points of cricket at all levels. The encouragement of sport, and the development of the necessary skills, at 'grass-roots' level has always been a conscious part of our sponsorship policy at NatWest. It is only from such small beginnings that we can expect to nurture and encourage future world-class sportsmen and women and also equip more people, far removed from the glitter of the world stage, to get greater enjoyment from their chosen sport.

The superb cricket witnessed in Australia during the 1986/7 tour by the England team, which reigned supreme, will, I hope, encourage more spectators to watch our national Summer sport and many more youngsters to take an active interest in the game, perhaps for the first time. Whether spectator, novice or coach I am sure you will find this *Guide to Better Cricket* a most useful addition to your bookshelf.

Boardman

PREFACE

*M*y colleagues could not resist chuckling when I told them I was writing a book about the game of cricket. 'Surely you are not going to advocate people playing cricket in the same way as you do?' – a fair point as anyone who has seen me bat or field will recognize immediately. Of course I'm not. The TCCB couldn't possibly endorse such an idea.

It may be more accurate to say that I've compiled rather than written this book. With tape recorder in hand I've sat down with some of the finest contemporary cricketers and asked them how they play the game, since I reasoned that the likes of Rod Marsh, Viv Richards, John Emburey and Joel Garner must have something to offer the rest of us. I hope that these conversations have resulted in a book that is neither too technical nor too dogmatic. In fact there were occasions when my 'experts' outlined contradictory approaches to the game. I've tried to highlight these differences rather than dilute them.

Every cricketer would love to be able to bowl like Dennis Lillee and bat like Viv Richards, but sooner or later we all discover that this is not possible. No two cricketers bat or bowl in the same way; all have individual technical quirks as well as different methods of preparing for a game. It would be foolish to encourage anyone to slavishly emulate one model. Anyone who wishes to improve must first discover his own strengths and weaknesses and build from there. Hopefully by reading about players of different styles and techniques you can discover a few fresh ideas and ploys that will hasten that improvement. Some may benefit more from observing Geoff Marsh rather than Viv Richards, Pat Pocock rather than John Emburey and vice versa. The idea is that you select from each what you think to be valuable rather than become a tepid clone of any one of the experts.

The players whom I interviewed were all remarkably generous with their time and extremely cooperative and I thank them for that. Often I accosted them at the most inconvenient times. Typically, David Gower was quite prepared to sit and chat even though he had just collected a 'pair' against Western Australia in England's final match before the first Test of the 1986/7 Ashes series. In such situations the last thing anyone wants to do is talk about batting but David, of course, was both courteous and helpful. In less trying circumstances so were the others. If ever they appear inarticulate it's because my batteries went flat. In other words, it's my fault.

The book is liberally illustrated with action photos; often these can be more instructive than the written word. Some of them show the players departing from textbook orthodoxy. The reason for this is that this is often what happens on the field. A Gower cover drive is a delight to behold but the dry technician might complain about the position of his right foot – it's not close enough to the ball. The fact is that Gower finds it much harder to hit the ball sweetly if his foot is where the textbook demands.

For those of you who are uncertain as to what constitutes textbook orthodoxy, there are some line drawings which describe the basic batting shots and the bowler's grips etc. I'm grateful to Keith Andrew of the National Cricket Association for preparing them. However one word of warning: don't be too alarmed if your cover drive doesn't quite mirror these drawings – provided you are making contact with the ball. The goal for all cricketers should be to be more effective and successful, not to look technically perfect. As Bradman points out in *The Art of Cricket* "If technique is going to prove the master of the player and not his servant, then it will not be doing its job."

As I was writing (or compiling) the book I asked my editor whom she thought it should be aimed at – club cricketers? – schoolboys? – coaches? It was a naïve question since she immediately responded 'anyone aged between 7 and 97 who is remotely interested in cricket'. I hope she is right. Ideally those who play the game, whether for the Under XI's or The Forty Club, will discover something new from the experts' contributions. Those who have passed on their kit to sons and grandsons or who now use their box as a receptacle for spare collar studs will, I hope, find it interesting as they sit in the stands or an armchair to have a glimpse of what goes through the minds of top class cricketers taking strike or starting their run ups. At the very least I hope those interviews have helped improve my own game.

Finally, I would like to thank all those who gave up their time to be interviewed; Tessa Rose for those inspiring telephone calls; and my wife for telling me to 'get on with it'.

Vic Marks, Tiverton, 1987

Vic Marks bowls for England

PREPARING
FOR THE
SEASON

'It is very important for a man who wishes to have a good season to take regular exercise.'

PRINCE RANJITSINHJI

A familiar sight at 10 am at County grounds throughout the country. The process would have mystified the likes of W.G., Woolley and Compton.

*T*he story goes that Denis Compton would make his first appearance at Lord's each year 20 minutes before the start of the opening County match of the season. He would stroll into the dressing room, slip on his flannels and borrow one of the junior professionals' bats, then he would stride out into the middle and score a century. I doubt whether he would be very interested in what follows in this chapter. For us normal mortals, however, some preparation is essential before an approaching cricket season. Unlike Denis Compton, we need to have confidence in our equipment, especially the bat, to feel fit and to have had some form of practice. Then, perhaps, we can convince ourselves that there is some chance of combating the deadly inswinging yorker that invariably greets us first ball each season or of clinging on to the steepling skier that has, inevitably, avoided the other ten fielders.

SELECTING KIT

For advice on equipment I talked to Andrew Kennedy. Andy, who was elected Young Cricketer of the Year in 1975, played for Lancashire for 10 years after qualifying as a teacher. He now coaches the boys (and girls) at Taunton School in Somerset as well as running the sports shop there. It's a far cry from his own cricketing origins, which are the cobbled back streets of the industrial north of England, followed by hours in the nets with the sympathetic local pro. While playing English County cricket he attended various coaching courses at Lilleshall, the national sports centre, where he progressed from preliminary to advanced. Finally he became a staff coach, teaching would-be coaches. He observes ruefully that he learnt more about coaching from the four weeks at Lilleshall than during a decade at Lancashire and he recommends the courses strongly.

Andy sells many bats to 10-year-olds or, to be more precise, to their fathers, and herein lies a problem. He explains: 'The parents always say "I want a bat that will last a couple of years" and they pick out one that comes up to his chin. This can ruin the youngster's prospects since he can scarcely lift the bat, let alone swing it.' It is crucial to select a bat of the right dimensions. The young player's heroes, such as Botham, Border and Lloyd, may use 3lb cudgels to such great effect that it is tempting to try to emulate them, but such a policy will prove disastrous for a beginner. Remind him that Don Bradman used a bat of less than 2½lb; if he doesn't know who Don Bradman is, tell him. Certainly ensure that the bat is neither too heavy nor too large and that he can swing it easily.

When professionals select a bat they go through two procedures. First, they bounce a ball up and down on it to check that the middle feels 'sweet'; then they adopt their normal stance and play a few imaginary drives to see whether it 'picks up well' and whether it is bottom heavy. The heaviest of bats can feel light if it is perfectly balanced. The optimum weight will usually be dictated by the size and strength of the batsman and by his technique. A batsman who specializes in booming straight drives will probably prefer a heavier bat, while someone who is adept at cutting and pulling will use a light one. Some players have recently started carrying bats of varying weights in their bags; for instance, Vivian Richards might begin his innings against the fast bowlers with one of his lighter bats before calling ominously for a heavier one when the unfortunate spinner comes into the attack.

Top class batsmen tend to develop their own variations. Clive Lloyd, for example, has six additional rubber grips on the handle of his bat. The thicker the handle, the lighter the bat picks up; Andy assures me that the reason for this has 'something to do with physics'. Whatever the reason, it's not an option for the young batsman, who should aim to select the right weight of bat at the outset in consultation with his teacher/coach, if appropriate. The size of the bat can also cause problems. For example, a short-handled bat can look incongruous when used by someone like Clive Lloyd, who is well over 6 feet tall, but it can be ideal for a smaller batsman. Again, it's a question of trying out equipment before you buy to find out what suits you best.

Once a bat of the right dimensions has been selected, there is still a wide array of choices. Is a traditional plain wood bat preferable to one with a polyarmoured or plastic coating? Most professionals use plain wood bats, which seem to hit the ball more crisply, but they usually have the luxury of an endless supply of free bats from the makers. These bats, however, no matter how tenderly they are oiled and 'knocked in', are more likely to crack, especially when

Trinidad, 1986 – Botham tests his armour before facing the West Indian speed quartet. In addition to the usual club cricketers' precautions in the shape of pads, gloves, thigh pad and box, he has a chest pad, an arm guard and a helmet. Facing such formidable opposition, who can blame him?

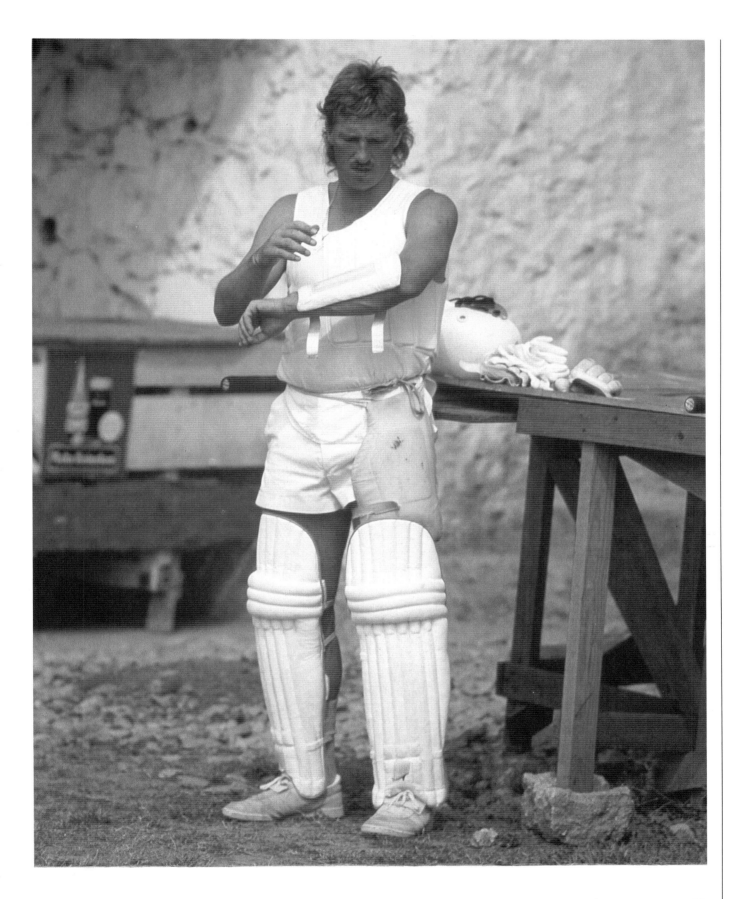

used with cheaper balls. Since cricket bats are very expensive, Andy Kennedy often advises the purchase of bats with an artificial covering. These require minimal maintenance – just a wipe with a damp cloth; they are often cheaper and they last longer.

One final point – selection shouldn't be rushed; it is a very important decision. Confidence in your bat brings a massive psychological advantage, for if you feel you don't have to hit the ball hard to reach the boundary you are more likely to prosper. Striving to hit the ball too hard can have dire consequences, whether you are on a tennis court, a golf course or a cricket pitch. Even seasoned County professionals with their immediate access to new equipment will lovingly tend and repair their favourite bat to keep it in operation for as long as possible.

Just as batsmen should devote special attention to their choice of bat so bowlers, particularly fast ones, should take great care with their footwear. On his first overseas tour to Australia in 1982/3 Norman Cowans threw two random pairs of new boots into his cricket 'coffin' before departure. Soon after his arrival he had innumerable problems with his feet. Bob Willis, a veteran of a dozen tours, was amazed at such naïvety and quickly acquired enough boots to fill another cricket coffin in the hope of finding a comfortable pair for his prospective fast bowling partner. Particularly on the hard, unyielding grounds of Australia, India and the West Indies, comfortable, well-fitting boots are vital.

Andy recommends high-ankled boots for fast bowlers, as he's witnessed an increase in injuries even among 12-year-olds wearing cricket shoes with little support. Most County fast bowlers opt for this type, though there are exceptions, notably John Lever of Essex, who prefers light studded shoes and who has consistently avoided injury over the years. For all but fast bowlers rubber-soled shoes have become more popular recently; they are fine on dry and artificial surfaces, but in wet conditions studded shoes are best for the prevention of injury and run outs.

The great Prince Ranjitsinhji, who played 15 times for England at the turn of the century, wrote in the *Jubilee*

Meanwhile, Ranji in 1896 requires less protection. His Jubilee Book of Cricket *is a fascinating historical document which also provides a wealth of good advice for young cricketers and remains one of the best books on the game. The basics of the game haven't changed that much since Ranji's heyday at the turn of the century.*

Book of Cricket: 'Always have a good-fitting pair of pads and gloves to save the limbs from pain and injury'. Of course that still applies, though the standard of the equipment has risen dramatically since then; a mysterious epidemic of broken fingers in 1986, however, has prompted glove manufacturers to rethink their designs. But Ranji would have been mystified by any discussion of helmets.

Ten years ago, when Dennis Amiss strode out for Warwickshire wearing a white motorbike helmet perched on top of his head and looking like an ageing Hell's Angel, many of his fellow pros couldn't resist a wry chuckle or two. Now it is an exceptional batsman who disdains to use the helmet; most of us pop it on our heads as automatically as we insert the box. Viv Richards regards the wearing of a helmet as an unnecessary encouragement to the bowler as well as a slight on his own manhood, but he is the only modern player who refuses to use it under any circumstances. In professional cricket now, opting not to wear a helmet against fast bowling is provocative, acting as a stimulus for the bowler to bowl quicker and shorter, something which most players prefer to avoid.

Andy Kennedy has never discouraged the use of helmets outside the first class game, whether in club or school cricket. Again there may well be some giggles and asides, but if they help the batsmen to be in a more confident frame of mind, as well as safer, they must be considered worthwhile. However he does concede that they are seldom necessary for 13-year-olds playing in their own age bracket since the ball should never reach head height.

In *The Art of Captaincy* former England captain Mike Brearley describes how the advent of the helmet helped his batting against the quicks. In pre-helmet days, he writes, 'There were indeed moments of fear. But near misses and the occasional blow do not so much produce fear as a lack of eagerness for further bombardment. My reaction was the cricketing equivalent of the stiff upper lip. I stood up behind the ball and took whatever punishment was coming. But I discovered that wearing the helmet enabled me to be less rigid in response, more varied, more playful, more creative. I was able to use a range of responses to the short pitched ball rather than only one. Richards may need to rein in his own adventurousness; ordinary mortals need every encouragement to be spontaneous'. Whether you possess the brains of Brearley or not, it's worth protecting them.

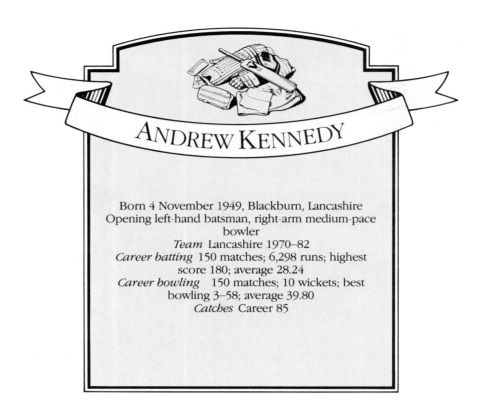

ANDREW KENNEDY

Born 4 November 1949, Blackburn, Lancashire
Opening left-hand batsman, right-arm medium-pace
bowler
Team Lancashire 1970–82
Career batting 150 matches; 6,298 runs; highest
score 180; average 28.24
Career bowling 150 matches; 10 wickets; best
bowling 3–58; average 39.80
Catches Career 85

PHYSICAL PREPARATION

In 1961, when the Worcestershire players reported back in April, Norman Gifford remembers that they changed straight into their flannels, wandered over to the nets and started practising. If the weather was wet they enjoyed a game of five-a-side football. Cricketers didn't even possess a tracksuit and fitness was achieved simply by bowling and batting in the nets plus the occasional fielding practice. Fifteen years later the scene had changed dramatically. The advent of one-day cricket, demanding fieldsmen to dive, twist and turn and batsmen to scamper twos and threes in quick succession prompted County sides to pay more attention to physical fitness. Eddie Barlow, for instance, captain of Derbyshire in the late Seventies, outlined a comprehensive winter training programme for all his players and cross-country runs became a regular feature of April's pre-season schedule. Not everyone welcomed the change. Mike Hendrick, when asked whether he thought the new regime was beneficial, wryly observed, 'If we come across a batsman who can smash the ball three miles, Derbyshire will be the first side in the County Championship to get it back.'

While arguments rage about the relative merits of cricketers of different eras, few deny that today they are fitter and more agile than in the past. The physio/trainer has become a constant companion/tormentor of international and County sides. I talked to one of this new breed, Dennis Waight, who hails from Sydney but who has accompanied the West Indies all around the world. During his time the West Indies have lost very few Test matches,

though Dennis does not take all the credit for that. He has also spent several summers with Somerset CCC, where results have fluctuated rather more.

In his youth (he refuses to be specific about dates) Dennis was more than proficient at several sports – rugby league, athletics, swimming and boxing – though, strangely, cricket was not one of them. A course in physiotherapy and physical education seemed to him a sensible option. When Kerry Packer shook the cricket world to its foundations by introducing World Series Cricket, he insisted that each side should have its own trainer. Dennis, given the choice between the Rest of the World XI and the West Indies, opted for the latter and so impressed them that he has been with them since 1977. He recognized that they were 'tremendous movers' but he thought that they could be fitter and even more flexible. Naturally this diminutive, craggy Australian received a few suspicious glances at the outset, but with the captain, Clive Lloyd, supportive and the benefits of his exercises becoming increasingly apparent, he gained the confidence of the whole squad within a year. Just as it's vital for a batsman to have confidence in his bat, so it's crucial for a player to have faith in his trainer.

Dennis defines his role in typically blunt terms: 'to get them fit, to keep them fit, to minimize injuries and to get the injured back on the field as quickly as possible'. However, he admits to becoming something of a 'mother

Andy Kennedy now has a more sedate life than when he was a top-class batsman and opened the batting for Lancashire. He is the cricket coach at Taunton School, Somerset, where he also runs the sports shop. During the holidays he skippers Dorset in the Minor Counties Competition – so he's a real enthusiast.

figure' as he gradually builds up relationships with his players. Presumably psychiatrists don't stick their patients on a couch for nothing, and Dennis finds that injured players, while receiving treatment, will often outline frustrations and doubts that they might not be happy airing to the captain or manager. As his rapport with the players develops, Dennis knows who to cajole and who to pander, who exaggerates an injury and who plays it down. Ultimately only the player can decide whether he should play in a game, but Dennis can prompt and explain the risks involved. He marvels at the resilience and determination of the West Indians, recalling in particular Malcolm Marshall batting and then bowling England out with a broken thumb in 1984.

I asked Dennis what would be the ideal preparation for a cricket season. His remarks were based upon an English County season. Even though club cricketers reading this may have neither the time nor the inclination to follow the routine strictly, they can adapt from his suggestions a programme of their own. Incidentally, when the Somerset players were informed of Dennis' appointment, we became a trifle apprehensive, fearing all kinds of physical torture. In fact the reality was quite tolerable. Dennis recognized early in his career that the requirements of cricketers are far removed from those of athletes, boxers or rugby players.

He points out that a reasonable level of fitness is important not only for bowlers, who obviously require stamina and endurance, but also for batsmen. Physical fitness goes hand in hand with mental fitness. Once you become tired you quickly lose concentration, with the usual fatal consequences. This is not a new discovery. Indeed, Ranji wrote in 1897: 'It is very important for a man

Dennis Waight, with the 'magic spray', calmly attends to a stricken Gordon Greenidge, while Courtney Walsh looks on with interest. The West Indians have complete confidence in their physio's skills and, as a result, he's twice as effective; 1st Test, W. Indies v England, Kingston, 1986.

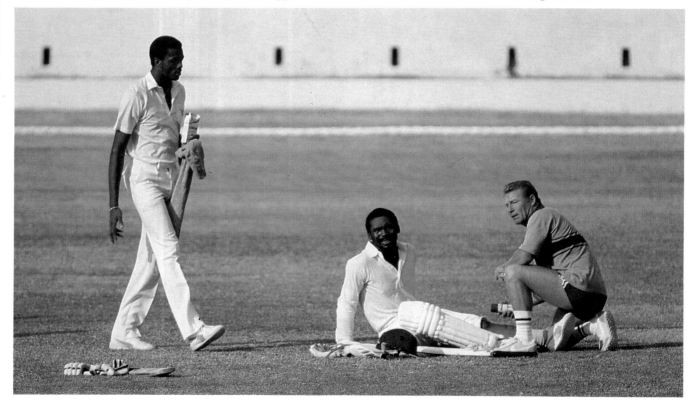

Somehow Waight managed to keep Clive Lloyd (foreground) going until his retirement in 1985, even though the West Indian captain 'had the knees of an octogenarian'.

who wishes to have a good season to take regular exercise during the winter months. Boys at school and men at university play football, racquets and fives. But there are many people, who play first class cricket during the summer, but during the winter take no exercise at all worthy of the name. This is a great mistake and leads to much bad form in the earlier part of the season.'

While Dennis would not disagree with that, not many of us have access to fives courts. Instead, he recommends some long-distance running to build up endurance and stamina before the season begins. It needn't be far: 3–3½ miles three times a week over a period of six to eight weeks is sufficient. He is reluctant to begin any sprint work before the basic training has been completed since, he says, 'If you sprint when unfit you run raggedly and pick up bad habits; your arms start to wobble all over the place and your legs don't come up high enough. I start my players sprinting at 80 per cent effort, hopefully with high knee lift and the arms pumping.' If only I'd been exposed to Dennis a little earlier in my career.

Gradually he introduces more short sprints, trusting that the endurance work can be catered for during net/fielding practice. In addition, and most importantly, there will be plenty of stretching exercises before and during each training session. Stretching is the central core of Dennis' work and he outlines its benefits as follows: 1, it simply makes you feel good; 2, it helps you to move more quickly and with greater flexibility; and 3, it reduces by 50 per cent the likelihood of injury from muscle tears. There are two possible methods – ballistic stretching, which involves a series of rapid movements, or static stretching. Dennis is a firm advocate of the static method, and both the West Indies and Somerset players will spend 10–15 minutes doing the exercises before every day's cricket.

First, it is important to get the blood pumping to the muscles. This can be achieved by jogging for a couple of minutes. Then it's simply a matter of holding the body in the various stretches for 25–30 seconds. The basic stretches exercise the calf muscles, hamstrings, thighs, groin, lower back, sides, shoulders and neck. All but the shoulders and neck, which should be rotated, require the body to be locked into position and stretched. Beginners should not work at maximum effort at the outset, but should build up slowly to accustom their bodies to the exercises. The soreness will still be there after a few days, but it wears off steadily as the muscles elongate. The result should be that on a bleak morning at the beginning of the season the player is less likely to pull a muscle. Dennis' work with the

West Indies and Somerset has convinced me that such precautions are worthwhile.

Exercising as a team may also enhance a player's mental preparation, since it creates a routine time when he can switch on to the challenges of the day; the exercises can function like a cricketing alarm clock. When locked in a hamstring stretch you can contemplate what sort of contribution you may be asked to make on that day and envisage the perfect outswinger or a flowing cover drive. If the exercises do nothing else they help to wake you up.

PRACTISING THE SKILLS

Norman Gifford, while recognizing the increased need for fitness in the modern game, is adamant that this should not be achieved at the expense of the practising of skills. After almost 30 years in the game, 15 as a County captain, and 3 tours as England's assistant manager, he should know. Golfers and tennis players may spend a few hours a week doing physical exercises but the bulk of their practice time will be spent on the links or on court polishing their game skills. Similarly, cricketers before a season or on tour should prepare predominantly with a bat or a ball in their hands; they will usually do this in the nets.

Ian Botham and Viv Richards combine forces to stretch their thigh muscles and limber up generally before a match – Torvill and Dean beware!

The goals of any net session are to rediscover and refine skills and to increase the confidence of the player. But beware; a poorly organized net practice on an indifferent surface can actually be detrimental to a player's game. For this reason, when on tour Gifford used to visit the available facilities the day before the scheduled practice so that he could plan the session in advance.

Good quality net wickets are essential. A batsman who is unsure whether the next ball will brush his nose or clatter his ankles will develop technical flaws as well as lose confidence, while the bowlers will depart with an exaggerated opinion of themselves. Cricket groundsmen are a much harassed breed, but it is worth flattering, badgering or bribing them to produce good net wickets as well as a decent square.

Let us assume that the conditions are ideal and that Norman Gifford is in charge of two nets. He prefers to have one fast net and one slow one. Many batsmen change their technique or use a different guard when playing fast bowlers as opposed to spinners, and it can upset their rhythm if they have to change styles every other ball.

With two different nets available, the batsmen can simply swap nets after 7–10 minutes instead.

Three bowlers in each net is sufficient; otherwise players become distracted, bored or, in England, cold, as they await their turn to bowl. Meanwhile the rest of the squad can either help by retrieving balls, or conduct their own fielding practice as well as being ready to replace the batters and bowlers in the nets.

Gifford lets his fast bowlers operate for about 45 minutes (the equivalent of 7–10 overs) and he insists that they bowl off their proper run ups. He detests the sight of front line bowlers 'filling in' off random run ups just to provide practice, as this is a breeding ground for bad habits; the arm tends to get lower, the run up ragged and rhythm, a bowler's most precious commodity, is easily destroyed. Once each fast bowler has finished his spell Gifford packs him off for a shower and a change of shirt so that he can return to bat and field later in the day. Spinners may want to bowl a little longer – and in my experience they are always required to anyway. All bowlers, particularly spinners with their greater variety of balls, should bowl with a purpose. At the beginning of a session, or indeed a season, they should concentrate on rediscovering their line and length and then start on specific goals, such as getting closer to the stumps or ensuring that the arm is as

Every picture tells a story. Karachi, 1978 – Geoff Boycott, regardless of the quality of the nets, is already hard at work when Downton, *Edmonds, Barrington and Miller arrive. To dismiss him in a net is as remarkable as getting him in the middle.*

high as possible. They may like to develop an away swinger or a yorker and several other variations. It is advisable, and often far less costly, to carry out these experiments in the nets rather than in the middle.

Since net practice is a long way removed from an actual game, considerable self-discipline and imagination are required, particularly from bowlers. Each bowler should have a clear mental picture of his field setting and it's a good idea to describe it to the batsman. On occasions it helps concentration to make an honest assessment of every ball you bowl so that you have some idea of your analysis at the end of the session. On the 1982/3 tour to Australia, the stalwart medium pacer Robin Jackman played very few first class games and was condemned to long spells in the nets, a potentially soul-destroying situation. The only way that he could check his form was by setting himself a target of 10 overs and monitoring every delivery. At the end of the session he would declare triumphantly that he had taken 5–31. (He was always the most optimistic of bowlers.) This assertion would be the

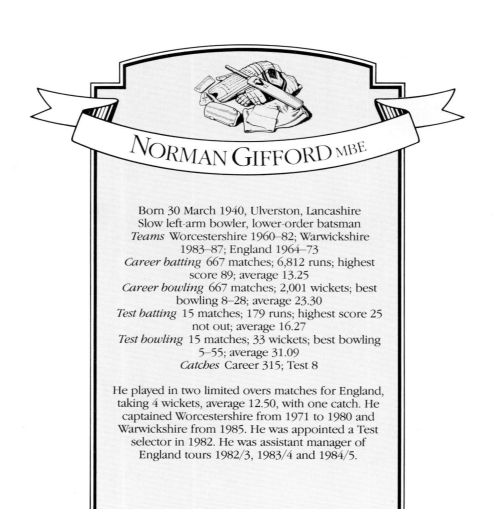

NORMAN GIFFORD MBE

Born 30 March 1940, Ulverston, Lancashire
Slow left-arm bowler, lower-order batsman
Teams Worcestershire 1960–82; Warwickshire
1983–87; England 1964–73
Career batting 667 matches; 6,812 runs; highest
score 89; average 13.25
Career bowling 667 matches; 2,001 wickets; best
bowling 8–28; average 23.30
Test batting 15 matches; 179 runs; highest score 25
not out; average 16.27
Test bowling 15 matches; 33 wickets; best bowling
5–55; average 31.09
Catches Career 315; Test 8

He played in two limited overs matches for England,
taking 4 wickets, average 12.50, with one catch. He
captained Worcestershire from 1971 to 1980 and
Warwickshire from 1985. He was appointed a Test
selector in 1982. He was assistant manager of
England tours 1982/3, 1983/4 and 1984/5.

cause of endless debate, but the important thing was that the whole exercise had heightened his concentration as well as his confidence.

In theory, batsmen should adopt the same self-disciplined attitude and they should be encouraged to do so; but in practice, at international level, Norman Gifford has seen several contrasting approaches to batting in the nets. Geoff Boycott bats as if it were the first 20 minutes of a Test Match; his game is based upon a rock solid defence and he wants to ensure that it is in perfect working order. I must admit that 20 minutes watching Boycott in a net could teach a young batsman far more than reading an entire coaching manual. In contrast, an attacking batsman like Allan Lamb has different requirements. He wants, in Gifford's words, 'to feel that his hands are right on the bat and to be sure that his timing is sweet'. Lamb needs to have confidence in his attacking shots and in a net he will forfeit the odd dismissal if he can hit the ball crisply. If he's unhappy at the end of his session, he'll probably go off into a vacant net and get someone to throw balls at him so that he can refine his timing. Provided this approach is not used as an excuse for indiscriminate slogging, it is no more irresponsible than Boycott's, even though it may seem so

at first sight. Remember, nets are not only to sharpen the technique but also to build up confidence for forthcoming matches.

Gifford, meanwhile, has been hovering at the back of the nets, cajoling and encouraging, alerting batsmen to pad up and replacing bowlers where necessary. Practising in the nets is not as much fun as playing and it helps if no time is squandered by a lack of organization so he tries not to interrupt the flow of the net, particularly with younger players. There's nothing worse for a batsman than having a fussy coach eroding chunks of that precious 15 minutes' batting time. Indeed, both Gifford and Kennedy are convinced that the first and most important role of the coach is to foster a young player's enjoyment, even love, of the game. Gifford says: 'We don't want young cricketers to finish school, rush to the nets and there be taken straight back to the classroom. Nets are not an examination and

Norman Gifford bowling for Worcestershire against Leicestershire in a Gillette Cup match 1973. He was considered something of a veteran then. In 1987 he was still playing – for

Warwickshire with enviable zest. These qualities persuaded the selectors that he would be ideal as assistant manager on England's tours: he fulfilled this role on three consecutive tours.

I'm extremely wary of coaches who are slaves to orthodoxy. Our first aim should be to encourage youngsters to enjoy the duel between batsman and bowler and to savour the thrill of hitting the ball or deceiving the batsman. It worries me that we have concentrated too much on the technical side rather than simply allowing young players to enjoy it.'

Once a youngster has developed a zest for the game he will want to learn and improve and it may well be a case of him badgering the coach for advice. However, it is best to restrict observations of a player's performance until he has finished his net. Outline his strengths as well as his weaknesses and offer suggestions for him to concentrate on in his next session. Avoid trying to remedy all his faults at once. One specific point, say picking the bat up earlier, is enough to work on in each session. Nor should unorthodoxy, if it is successful, be discouraged. I have winced when witnessing a young batsman whip an off stump half volley superbly through mid-wicket only for the coach to meander down the track explaining the dangers of the shot. What if somebody had done that to Viv Richards twenty years ago?

Modern technology, in the shape of the bowling machine and the video recorder, has broadened the scope of practice. The bowling machine is especially useful in ironing out one particular flaw because, unlike human beings, it can be programmed to bowl in just about the same place ball after ball. So if you are struggling with your off drive, it is possible to practise that shot exclusively for 10 minutes, and to enable the necessary body movements to become automatic. I find one drawback with these machines: my body cheats by moving into position before the ball is released. However, I expect readers of this book to display greater self-discipline.

The video recorder is sparsely used in professional cricket, to my surprise; yet a recording can outline your flaws far more easily than a conversation with the coach. Human nature dictates that we're never totally convinced by other people's criticisms of our play: it is more difficult to argue with a video recording. It is equally useful to have a recording of yourself playing well, preferably in a match. You may be able to spot one small point that contributes to good form; in addition, a visual reminder that you have been a successful player can cast aside the attractions of premature retirement when you are in the doldrums.

One final thought for captains and selectors; be wary of judging players solely on their performances in nets. Such accomplished players as David Gower and Derek Randall have rarely looked convincing within the confines of a net, yet their records in the middle speak for themselves. Similarly, fast bowlers tend to bowl off 18 yards and often seem impressively quick. Try to get them back if you can, but in my experience it's an impossible task.

An increasingly popular alternative to net practice, at least at County level, is to practise in the middle, the only drawback being that it is a very time-consuming exercise. Two bowlers operate from the same end while two batsmen who are likely to bat together in a match play for approximately 25 minutes. The false sense of security often created by nets is now removed; running between wickets is sharpened and no balls should be completely eliminated. Targets may be set for pairs of batsmen and match situations more easily created. Time and patience are required, but middle practice proves a welcome diversion from being enclosed in a net. England batsmen on tour are, after a month of exclusive nets, prone to nightmares about receiving their first ball in the middle; they envisage hitting it, running after it and then throwing it back to the bowler.

When on tour Norman Gifford took the fielding practices and enjoyed doing so; even better, we enjoyed them as well. His main concern was to make them interesting and a challenge. He says:

'I could hit balls straight to fielders like David Gower and Allan Lamb and they would catch them 99 times out of 100, so I try to create a match situation where they have to run at full stretch before completing the catch. The hardest part in catching is balancing yourself and keeping your head still, and that's obviously trickier when you're on the move. After all, how many little lollipops do you get during a season? There are far more half chances and I like to simulate them and to nurture the philosophy that you go for everything.'

In a group of half a dozen Norman will hit four or five balls in succession to the same fielder, running him left and right, backwards and forwards while the others spectate, applaud and jeer. The fieldsman is 'on stage' for about 45 seconds and a competitive element is introduced between the group. The whole process can be physically demanding and is an excellent alternative to mindless running.

The Australians practise their slip catching technique in the Nursery at Lord's; 1975. Slip catching is usually accomplished by a batsman nicking balls that are thrown at him into a slip cordon. This method of practice produces far more realistic catches than those coming from the face of the bat.

Gifford is quick to assess the capabilities of his fielders; the catches for Pocock and, sad to relate, Marks, require less running than those for Randall or Botham, but everyone is stretched to his limit. He never lets anyone finish with a dropped catch, just as a showjumper who has been eliminated will pop his horse over one of the easier fences before leaving the ring. Again, confidence is a crucial factor and on match days the catches may be a little less demanding. He wants fieldsmen to be hungry for the ball. When a catch goes up they should be thinking 'It's in the air, that's out', rather than 'Oh my goodness, this one's coming to me'.

Slip catching is no longer practised with the coach in his blazer hitting catches from the face of the bat to a semi-circle of fielders. Instead, one man throws the ball at a batsman, who nicks it to a slip cordon. These catches are less predictable and more realistic. The personnel in the slip cordon should resemble the likely combination in a match; however, at some point it's worth everyone having a go, as another Bobby Simpson may be discovered.

Limited overs cricket has increased the value of fieldsmen being able to shatter the stumps with a direct hit; a run out can change the course of any game, so it's worth paying attention to shying at the stumps. A simple procedure is to erect two stumps a wicket's length apart and to divide the group into two. Behind one stump is the wicketkeeper, plus half the fieldsmen; he rolls the ball in the direction of extra cover and a fielder picks it up and hurls it at the other stump before joining the second group. Meanwhile, a member of the second group backs up and returns the ball to the wicketkeeper; this fielder will then jog to the wicketkeeper's group. The players continue to rotate at the whim of the coach or until the stump is reduced to a collection of splinters. Again, this exercise should improve marksmanship as well as taking some of the drudgery out of running.

By now, we should be ready for the first game of the season.

THE
RUN SCORERS

'Dominating a fast bowler is a joy – one of the best parts of batting.'

VIV RICHARDS

If you took a poll among current cricketers as to who has been the greatest batsman of the last decade, I think Viv Richards would win.

If you ever watch a group of children starting an impromptu game of cricket, the quarrels begin when it is time to decide who bats first. Batting is the most obviously attractive element of the game. When the amateurs used to present themselves to their County sides in July and August, the professionals soon discovered that they were nearly all batsmen and, no doubt, Ranji echoed the views of his peers when he wrote that batting 'is the most fascinating and delightful part of cricket'.

The batsman is the focal point of a cricket match; he has the starring role for as long as he remains at the crease. In those far-off days before televised cricket my father used to go to Taunton, not to see Somerset win (he was too much of a realist for that) nor to see Bedser bowl, but to watch Hammond, Compton or Hutton bat; a certain spice was added to the day by the knowledge that they might be dismissed first ball. Even now middle-aged cricket followers can be divided into those who did or did not see Bradman bat and today, despite the advent of the television which makes our heroes and heroines so familiar, the spectator still shuffles to the edge of the seat when Gower, Botham or Richards walk to the wicket.

For cricketers, the feeling of hitting a ball effortlessly to the cover boundary is truly wonderful – perhaps comparable to a golfer sending a 4 iron to within three feet of the flag or a tennis player executing a perfect lob; maybe, though I'm guessing now, a darts player hitting the treble 20. Apart from enjoying this sensation, batsmen have two other, more basic, aims. The first is not to be dismissed by the opposition; the second is to score runs, the quicker the better. The methods by which they achieve these goals can vary enormously. Brian Bolus, an opening batsman for England as well as Yorkshire, Nottinghamshire and Derbyshire, used one of the largest pairs of pads I've ever seen to aid survival. Harry Pilling (5 feet 3 inches), once of Lancashire, would square cut balls that Tony Greig (6 feet 8 inches) would cover drive. An off stump half volley might be driven through extra cover by Barry Richards but mid-wicket by Viv. All players, while observing the same rudimentary principles of the game, bat in different ways and I hope that some of these contrasts will be illustrated by the Test players I've spoken to in this chapter.

They began their cricketing lives in contrasting parts of the globe: Dar es Salaam, the outskirts of the Somerset market town of Yeovil, Antigua, Wandering, a small town 100 miles south of Perth, Western Australia, and Accring-ton, Lancashire. The cricket buffs reading this will probably have identified most of the players already. They are David Gower, Ian Botham, Viv Richards, Geoff Marsh and Graeme Fowler. The first three are regarded as being among the greatest players of this or any other era; they are instinctive batsmen, blessed with enormous natural ability. Marsh and Fowler may be less gifted, but through a more technical and analytical approach to their art have been good enough to open the batting for their countries. At the time of writing Fowler, after a topsy-turvy two years, is confined to Lancashire CCC while Marsh, after an excellent series against England in 1986/7, was appointed vice captain of Australia. It seemed sensible to balance the three instinctive players with two less eye-catching, less superhuman batsmen.

THE FORMATIVE YEARS

Everyone now knows that the first few years of life are the formative ones and from my own experience this applies also to cricket. In our garden there was a thick privet hedge at square cover which conveniently stopped the ball; at mid-wicket, however, there was a large greenhouse, so it was best to hit the ball towards cover point whenever possible. Twenty years later I still find that I can't hit the ball to mid-wicket and even projected on-drives end up at square cover.

Indeed, a large proportion of cricketers begin their lives in the backyard or on the lawn with long-suffering members of their family. Gower, at the age of four, was lobbed tennis balls by his father and mother so that he was well prepared for his first organized game, aged seven. His father was a 'proper cricketer' who could be relied upon for sound advice, while his mother had the wisdom to permit the young David to bat left handed.

He is thankful that as his career progressed he managed to avoid 'destructive' coaching. 'Both at school (King's Canterbury) and at Leicester people tended to encourage rather than remodel me; they were impressed enough to say, "You're naturally a good striker of the ball, keep that going; just tighten up a little here and there and learn to bat for longer".'

In Antigua, Viv Richards began with plenty of paternal encouragement and a bat made up from spare bits of wood. He was given his first real bat by a neighbour who

PREPARATION: GRIP, STANCE AND BACKLIFT

The artworks in this chapter depict the orthodox techniques of batting, beginning with the grip (right), the stance (below left and middle) and the backlift (below right). All players, including the great ones, depart from the textbook now and again so don't worry if you do as well, especially if you're scoring runs. Bradman, Viv Richards and Boycott all held the bat differently. But what should not be forgotten is that, such subtle variations apart, all of the great batsmen past and present had a solid foundation to their game, which is what the orthodox techniques provide.

The Grip The hands are held close together towards the top of the handle, with the fingers and thumbs curled well round.

The V's formed by forefinger and thumb are in line, and pointing between the outside edge of the bat and the splice.

The Stance The head is up, the eyes are level, and the leading shoulder is pointing towards the bowler. The knees are slightly flexed. This side-on view shows the feet positioned parallel to and either side of the crease. The bat is behind the toes of the back foot. The weight is on the balls of the feet. Alternatively (right), the bat can be held off the ground – a stance that enables tall batsmen to keep their eyes level and their view of the line of the ball clear.
Backlift (above) The bat is taken back straight over the stumps.

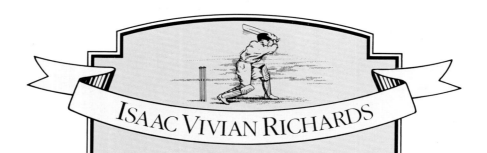

Isaac Vivian Richards

Born 7 March 1952, St Johns, Antigua
Attacking middle-order right-hand batsman, right-
arm off-break (occasional medium-pace) bowler
Teams Leeward Islands 1971/2 to 1986/7; Somerset
1974–86; Queensland 1976/7; West Indies 1974/5 to
1986/7
Career batting 397 matches; 29,061 runs; highest
score 322; average 49.67
Test batting 88 matches; 6,472 runs; highest score
291; average 52.61
Catches Career 363; Test 85

Regarded generally as the world's best batsman in
the mid-1980s, he is also a useful change bowler in
all types of cricket. He took over as captain of the
West Indies in 1984/5. He has scored 5,196 runs
(highest 189 not out), average 53.02, with 62
catches, in 131 limited overs matches for the West
Indies. His run aggregate is a world record. He left
Somerset controversially when not retained for the
1987 season, and joined Rishton in the Lancashire
League.

used to play for Antigua and he treasured the gift:

> *'Because he gave it to me, it was something special
> and I thought that I could play like him. Since it was a
> full-sized bat it was much too heavy, but I still went for
> hooks regardless. We played on rough, earthy surfaces
> that you wouldn't dream of playing cricket on in
> England or Australia. My father always encouraged
> me a lot but no one ever told me to cut any shot out,
> which is maybe why I play in a different way. Balls on
> middle stump I whacked through mid-wicket and
> there were no coaches to say "stop that".*
>
> *'Frank Worrell did come to the island once but it
> was more of a goodwill visit than a coaching exercise.
> It was an inspiration to see him, but I can't remember
> much of what he said. It was only when I went to Alf
> Gover that I discovered that cricket was a complicated
> game.'*

Richards, along with fellow Antiguan Andy Roberts,
spent some time at Gover's cricket clinic in London; it was
a mysterious experience for them both. They shivered
together, grew homesick together and yet both managed
to resist the temptation of a flight home.

> *'He [Gover] suggested changing my grip and having
> my elbow pointing in a different direction, and he
> talked about "playing straight". At the time it all
> meant nothing to me, but looking back I realize that I
> picked up something of value. Gover taught me to
> close the gap between bat and pad when defending. "I
> don't want to see any daylight," he kept saying. I
> didn't let him tamper with my attacking shots; they
> were already there, but he helped improve my defence.'*

So, even in his teens, Richards was mature enough to
pick out those snippets of advice which helped, while
ignoring much else. This is a very important skill, especially
for gifted players who, simply because they are so outstanding, attract advice in the same way that beer attracts
Australians. However, Richards' technical confusion
stretched into his Somerset career. An eager Phil Slocombe
once asked him where he formed his V's on the grip of his

*Richards hooks. When he
arrived at Taunton in 1974 this
was the shot that most impressed
his new colleagues, since it
requires superb reflexes and
great confidence to play it well.
It became an unequivocal
statement to the bowler. Later,
when everyone knew how good
he was, he used the shot less.*

THE RUN SCORERS 31

bat (that is, the V's formed by the thumb and forefinger of each hand when holding the bat) and Richards didn't know what he was talking about. Richards adopted the stance and grip that he did solely because he felt comfortable with them.

It can be dangerous for a coach to be dogmatic about such things. Bill Andrews, one of Somerset's most colourful characters, was once readjusting a pupil's grip when the young boy piped up, 'But Mr Andrews, this is how Bradman used to hold the bat.' An unimpressed Andrews replied, 'Well, just think how many runs he'd have scored if he'd held the bat properly.' It's a good story, though I doubt whether Andrews himself was a stickler for orthodoxy; certainly Bradman wasn't. In *The Art of Cricket* he points out that 'If technique is going to prove the master of the player and not his servant, then it will not be doing its job.' He then goes on to give us two examples that relate to his own batting style and which form an assault upon inflexible coaches. 'There are coaches who insist that every drive shall be made after the ball passes the front leg. I wish some coach could show me how to play an on drive that way – I can't do it.' On the subject of the straight backlift, much beloved by the textbooks, he says 'Mine wasn't and if I had been compelled to take my bat back on a perfectly straight line when intending to play the pull shot, I could never have done it.' A long line of English captains from A.P.F. Chapman to Norman Yardley would have slept more soundly if Bradman had been taught a straight backlift.

Richards, referring to the arc between mid-off and mid-on, makes a similar point:

> 'If you look to hit the ball in the V all the time, you'll never score any runs against a good bowler and tight field placements. If everyone follows the coaching books precisely, they'll be maidens every over. In my arsenal, I have the ability to hit through the leg side wide of mid-on; that's much more lucrative, though less correct.'

The above is not meant to be an attack upon coaching – rather upon dogmatic, inflexible coaching that worships orthodoxy and technical excellence for its own sake. I don't suppose this is a new problem since Ranji observed that 'there is a tendency among modern coaches to lay down fixed rules and advise all beginners to follow them without discrimination'. I fear that this tendency is still with us and lingers on.

Pakistan's captain, Imran Khan, executes a flowing cover drive as England wicketkeeper Bob Taylor looks on. His head is well balanced and his front foot has moved toward the ball, but there is still room for him to swing the bat freely.

Perhaps it is appropriate that a cricket coach should be introduced into the text at this point, if only to defend his trade. Daryl Foster has been the coach of the highly successful Western Australian State side for the last decade and his players would undoubtedly regard his contribution as being constructive.

Daryl believes that batting is perhaps the most difficult art in any sporting field, since one mistake can result in six hours of sitting in the pavilion. 'Batting is concerned with making runs, not looking good or being technically correct. There have been plenty of players who are technically well-nigh perfect, but who don't use their brains and therefore don't get the runs that their technique demands. Indeed, a so-called "technical deficiency" need not necessarily be an area of weakness; it only becomes that if a batsman is being regularly dismissed; then it is time for remedial action.' So Foster is not the sort of coach who

Off/On Drives

Batsmen play front foot drives to balls that are bowled to a full length. The illustrations show the off or cover drive and the finish of the on-drive

The backlift is high. The head and front shoulder lead on to the line of the ball.

Contact! The ball is struck with the full face of the bat. The weight is on the front foot – there is no pivot on the back foot.

A full follow through with good balance.

A short stride helps the batsman maintain his balance for the finish of the on-drive.

FORWARD LEG GLANCE

Unless your name is Ranjitsinhji, only play the leg glance to balls that are missing the leg stump.

The leading shoulder dips slightly as the front foot lands in line with the ball.

The ball is met in front of the pads. The wrists turn the blade of the bat on impact.

The head and trunk are kept ahead of the front pad. The aim is square and there is no falling away of the body to the off side.

BACKWARD LEG GLANCE

Right The top hand controls the bat, bringing it down close to the body.

Far right The balance is forward as the rising ball is pushed away.

would object to Richard's whip through mid-wicket or Gower's lack of foot movement when driving. Rather, he would delight in those shots.

When working with teenage batsmen, Foster encourages them to hit the ball. 'It is relatively easy for a coach to introduce a few technical refinements to a player who can hit the ball, but it's a devil of a job to get a technical, over-coached player to strike the ball cleanly and to widen his range of scoring shots.'

Of course, he concedes that a young player should start from a sound foundation, which begins with a comfortable stance with feet reasonably spaced and the bat resting against the front thigh: then he needs to master the drives (straight, off and on) and to be able to score behind the wicket on the off and leg side. To achieve this Foster regards the position of the head as crucial.

'Even in the stance too many people can't keep their balance because they have their head too far over to the off side. The head should be kept still and then moved to allow the batsman to get the best appreciation of the line and length of the ball. Footwork then becomes important, but mostly as a vehicle for getting the head in the optimum position. In fact, I think that there's been far too much emphasis placed on the bat and pad being locked together when the batsman is driving. If bat and pad are too close then it's impossible for the player to swing the bat properly and he hasn't the freedom to exert maximum force upon the ball. If you watch some of the great players like Ian Botham, Dean Jones and Clive Lloyd driving, their feet are usually in a good position but there is often daylight between bat and pad, while their heads are giving them the best possible viewing platform to hit the ball.'

When he is working with more mature cricketers, Foster believes that their mental approach can be of greater importance than their technique. At State or County level most players will have an established and, presumably, sound technique that it is too late to overhaul. Sometimes he asks a batsman to write down his approach to batting – which shots he is capable of playing, which shots he is working on and keen to improve and which shots he can't play. This little exercise may help the coach marginally but, more importantly, it should clarify in the batsman's mind how he intends to score his runs.

I would guess that this shot gave Geoff Boycott more pleasure than any other in his career. This clinical on-drive off a ball from Greg Chappell brought Boycott his 100th hundred in first class cricket. What better way to achieve this great distinction than during a Test match against Australia on your home ground? Leeds, 1977.

Flaws sometimes creep into even a batsman's favourite shot – let's say the off-drive – and when that happens Foster encourages the batsman to practise that particular shot on a bowling machine or by simply having off stump half volleys thrown at him. 'A golfer, if his 5 iron is not working properly, will go out and hit 200 5 irons until he's back in the groove. A batsman should try to do the same.'

It is relatively easy to spot defects but much harder to offer remedies, and Foster develops different checklists for different players. He tries always to spot the flaw at its earliest point, so initially he might check the position of the head in the stance or the movement of the feet – do they move too early? Do they always go to the same spot? He is anxious to go back to the root of the problem and uses a tennis player with an unreliable serve as an example. 'Often the problem may stem from a poor toss of the ball rather than the arching of the back or the follow through. In the same way one relatively minor adjustment early in the process can make all the difference to a batsman.'

He gives one example. Mike Veletta, Western Australia's opening batsman, is not well known in England, but he may well be by the end of the decade; he has toured India with Australia without playing a Test and had a prolific season in 1986/7 in the Sheffield Shield. During that season half of his dismissals were from catches down the leg side off the quicker bowlers. This happened because Mike's back foot went a long way to the off side as the bowler bowled (being an opener, Veletta is very keen to cover that danger area around off stump). The problem stemmed not from a poor execution of the leg glance but from his initial back foot movement, so Daryl discussed with him the two alternatives – either to restrict his initial foot movement or to stop attempting to play the leg glance. Foster sees his role as helping Veletta to identify the problem, while it is up to Veletta himself to choose the course of action. 'The best coach is the player himself; my position at State level is simply to offer observations and suggestions.'

In fact, Foster has spent a lot of time doing just that with Geoff Marsh. Geoff began on the farm playing mini-Tests with his brother. Later, at school in Perth, he revealed that he had exceptional talent and after his first Shield appearance in 1978 at the age of 19 a bright future in Australian cricket was taken for granted. It wasn't until the 1983/4 season, however, that he became firmly established in the State side as innings laced with brilliant stroke-play were interspersed with a frustrating run of failures. Those lean years persuaded Marsh to restrict his stroke-play and gave him the determination not to let his international career follow the same undulating pattern as his State career.

For the last fourteen years Marsh has used a personal coach, which is an unusual arrangement among first class cricketers. After a Test match Marsh still returns to him: 'He's prepared to put in time, which is special these days – mostly throwing balls at me and tightening my technique. I always feel good after I've had a session with him and my confidence rises. He watches me on TV and tells me if my feet are in the wrong position. I listen to him, but in the end I have to make my own decisions as to whether I change my method, since I'm the one who has to go out there.' Geoff is another example of a good player being selective in the advice he takes.

Graeme Fowler opened the batting for Accrington in the Lancashire League at the age of 15, when his first opponent was Australian international Neil Hawke. Also in the League

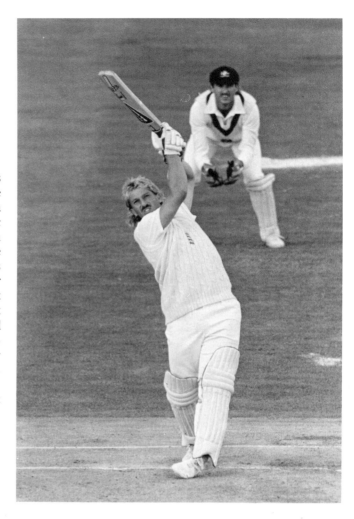

Botham launches a full-scale assault on the Australians. Whereas most of us do not even contemplate hitting fast bowlers back over their heads, Botham sets no limitations on what he can achieve. He gives himself the freedom to succeed – or fail – spectacularly. On this occasion he succeeded – spectacularly.

at that time were Dennis Lillee and Sarfraz Nawaz, so it could have been a harsh baptism. His captain let him open the batting with these instructions: 'You can have the first 10 overs (8 ball overs) to do what you want; if you're scoring runs, carry on; if you're not, get out.' Graeme graduated through the various Lancashire youth teams and the Second XI until he played in the first team as a No. 6 batsman and an occasional wicketkeeper. Within three years he was opening the batting for England. Interestingly, when he first appeared for Lancashire he was regarded as a 'hitter'.

This description could also be accurately applied to a young Ian Botham. He admits that he started 'trying to hit the ball everywhere'. Since 1974 he reckons he has made just two adjustments: 'Now my defence is as good as most; also, if I get to 50 then there's a good chance that I'll make

100; then I'll enjoy myself.' Of course what Botham should say, and what Boycott, Gavaskar or Marsh would say, is 'I dig in for another century'. But if he enjoys himself, then so do those watching.

From our five batsmen, we can see a pattern in their development emerging. All started with the ability to play a wide range of attacking shots (as Foster prefers) and from this base they have improved their defence and become slightly less daring in their shot selection. They have 'tightened up' in varying degrees, ranging from Botham, who has checked his natural instinct to belt the ball just a little, to Geoff Marsh, who has laid greater emphasis upon occupation of the crease, even if it is at the expense of a few attacking shots.

Gower observes that 'While everyone needs a straight bat and a sound defence, the better players around the world have a full range of attacking shots and they score quickly. They learn their attacking shots first and then acquire a sound defence. Even Chris Tavaré, as a schoolboy, was a prolific and speedy run scorer; it's just that he reined himself in earlier than most.' This is the most common path for a top class batsman.

There have been a few who have taken the opposite and, perhaps, more difficult route. They have concentrated first upon a rock solid defence and then gradually expanded their range of shots. The most dramatic example I can think of is Worcestershire and New Zealand opener Glenn Turner, who began his career as the dourest opener imaginable, but who was capable of scoring 311 in a day against Warwickshire in 1982. I regard this as a braver route to the top, since the young player who scores slowly is often more prone to failure and criticism early in his career than his dashing counterpart. Either way is fine, but it is up to the individual to decide whether his game will have more in common with Geoff Boycott or Chris Tavaré than David Gower or Ian Botham.

LIMBERING UP

In the first chapter we noted how batsmen prepare for a season with a series of net sessions. I have to report that neither Gower, Richards nor Botham enjoy prolonged sessions in the nets: admittedly one reason for this is that the cricket calendar now has so few gaps in it that these days there must be a far greater chance of international

After successful series' against India and England, Dean Jones has established himself as Australia's No. 3. He exudes confidence and aggression while at the crease and an eagerness to dominate the bowlers. It is unusual for such an attacking player to grip the bat so low on the handle. 5th Test, Australia v England, Sydney, 1987.

cricketers going stale rather than losing their touch.

When Richards used to enjoy the luxury of a lay-off before a season or a tour, he did a lot of running. Since he regards a strong wrist as an important element in his batting, he would also get a rubber ball and squeeze it until his wrists were tired. Then, in his room, he might throw the ball against the wall, thereby creating a range of catches for himself. At practice, using a cricket ball, he would spend a lot of time catching:

'Not straight catches but to the left, right, left, right, always focusing on the ball and catching one-handed. I'm sure this helps my reflexes. When I'm catching the ball well, I'm batting well. For me, that catching practice can be as useful as a net in ensuring that I'm keeping my eyes on the ball all the time. I'm not

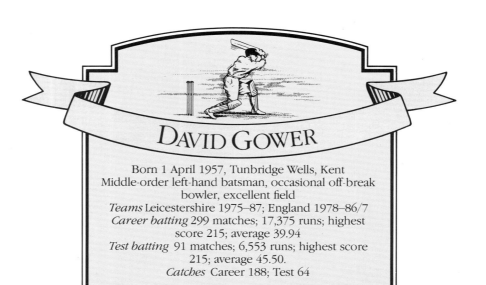

DAVID GOWER

Born 1 April 1957, Tunbridge Wells, Kent
Middle-order left-hand batsman, occasional off-break
bowler, excellent field
Teams Leicestershire 1975–87; England 1978–86/7
Career batting 299 matches; 17,375 runs; highest
score 215; average 39.94
Test batting 91 matches; 6,553 runs; highest score
215; average 45.50.
Catches Career 188; Test 64

He is considered the leading English batsman of the
mid-1980s. Having captained England in one Test
match in 1982, he assumed the regular captaincy in
1983/4, but was relieved of the task in 1986 after 21
Tests. He has played 99 limited overs matches for
England, scoring 2,855 runs (highest 158), average
32.07, with 38 catches.

particularly anxious to pick up a bat and I don't use nets too often; I'm a little paranoid about being enclosed. While batting, I love to see where my ball goes. If you hook in a net, the ball often comes back into your face. However, when I do use the nets, I try to bat as if I were in the middle; but if I'm in good nick, I won't have many sessions there.'

The same applies to Gower and Botham. Gower, like most of us, needs to feel confident before an innings:

'If I'm in good touch all I want is to have a few balls thrown to get my eyes, hands and feet linked up and to feel the bat coming through straight. If I'm out of nick then I'll have to work harder and have a net. If one area of my game is causing trouble, I'll ask the bowlers to concentrate there for five or ten minutes and then I'll finish with an all-round net so that I'm used to reacting to different types of deliveries.'
'Any other preparation?'
'I always like to be at the right ground on the right day.'

Botham, when in the nets, like Boycott bats just as he does in the middle; in his case, that means trying to smash 50 per cent of balls back over the bowler's head into the car park.

Our three middle order batsmen, unlike the openers (whom we shall observe shortly), have to endure the agonizing experience of waiting to bat. Gower, who has spent much of his career at No. 3, might be called to the wicket at 11.31am or 3.31pm; such uncertainty has no real parallel in sport. It is a time when anxieties and fears can haunt most devastatingly. Batting at 3, Gower will be ready at the start of the match and naturally he'll watch the opening overs to check conditions. But when he's done that, he doesn't watch in detail since 'others often make it look harder'.

From my observation, as well as personal experience, the longer a player has played, the less he watches. Constant spectating can be mentally draining, so players often seek some distractions – a newspaper, a crossword, a gossip, a fly on the wall. If anyone questions such a laid back approach, 'preserving mental energy' is the response.

In most dressing rooms, a familiar cycle develops. For example, a No. 7 batsman is usually relaxed and jovial at the start of the innings; he's pleased that the captain's won the toss and he may linger in the dressing room chatting, drinking tea, reading Bernard Levin. The first two wickets to fall are not a cause of great alarm to him. When the third wicket goes, however, he makes sure that all his kit is ready and he may put on his box and thigh pad, prompted no doubt by the recurring cricketer's nightmare about being summoned to face the hat-trick ball with your pads nowhere to be seen. Now he'll watch the game a little more closely and make a few inquiries about the quality of the wicket and the bowling. At the fall of the fourth wicket he

David Gower can even duck elegantly. Here he avoids a bouncer from Australia's Craig Mcdermott at Trent Bridge (1985). Evading bouncers and leaving the ball often demand as much skill and can give as much satisfaction as hitting the ball. Here, note how Gower's position allows him to keep an eye on the ball just in case it bounces irregularly.

puts his pads on and he may enter the 'condemned cell', the description which the black humorists in the side have given the seat in which the next batsman sits. At this point some stay silent and motionless, while others laugh and joke and gabble and leap around playing imaginary shots; after several false alarms, a wicket falls and the period of waiting is over.

Viv Richards prefers a relaxed and peaceful environment before batting, and he does not like to listen to a lot of comments. Too often he's seen a dismissed batsman return to the pavilion and remonstrate with his colleagues, 'I thought you said that this guy only bowled inswingers.' Last year that may well have been the case, but over the winter he may have developed an away swinger. Richards chooses 'to work it out for myself when I get out there' rather than be influenced by dressing room advice.

He will make a few basic observations which might affect his approach to his innings, however. For instance, he'll check the size of the boundaries, particularly in the area behind square leg, since they could dictate his use of the hook shot.

'When I'm hooking in front of the wicket, I'm in control and the size of the boundary is irrelevant, but if I'm hooking behind square, I can't be totally in control of where the ball goes and whether it's in the air or not. So at Taunton, with its short boundaries, I'm reasonably confident of clearing them; but at The Oval or the Melbourne Cricket Ground I'm not, so I'll be sure to avoid that shot.'

Greg Chappell hooks against England in 1982. During the series he was out several times hooking, but the shot also brought him many runs. He must have decided that the risk was worth taking. 3rd Test, Adelaide.

The direction of the wind is always worth checking (in fact, a familiar pose of Geoff Boycott when striding out to the wicket is the hoisting of his white handkerchief so that he can assess the breeze). What you imagine is a sweet lofted drive can turn into a swirling catch if it is played directly into the wind; meaty hooks just fail to clear deep backward square leg. A strong wind should also affect a batsman's running between the wickets. In Perth there is always 'one for the throw' when the fieldsman is throwing into a strong sea breeze; on the other side of the ground this would be suicide.

The speed of the outfield is also worth noting to save the embarrassment of playing a majestic cover drive and casually patting down the wicket only to see the ball come to a halt 3 inches short of the rope without a run having been scored.

Finally, the worst time to be waiting to bat is when a very quick bowler is bowling very fast. The situation is easily exacerbated if you have some colleagues nearby mumbling things like, 'I'd never have seen that one; that was quick; that would have hit me on the head; if only it was a decent batting surface, it would be all right.' Such depressing remarks can seriously undermine a batsman's confidence and thereby his game; consequently they should never be heard in a positive, purposeful dressing room.

PLAN FOR OPENERS

At least the openers are spared that dressing room torture. It is one of the advantages of the job, but there are others, which Graeme Fowler outlines:

'Usually there are few outfielders and the ball is harder, so if you're hitting the ball crisply there's no-one to stop it. Remember, too, that the bowlers are warming up at the same time as you, and that's why I like facing the first ball because it's often a bad one. Psychologically, it's an even contest between the batsman and bowler at the beginning of an innings. At No. 3 or 4 the pressure's usually on when you arrive at the crease; the bowlers, having just taken a wicket, are confident and in their rhythm.'

However, there are disadvantages as well: the new ball tends to move more in the air and off the wicket; it bounces more and travels faster. As a result, the opener has to be able to react quickly and be patient; indeed, one of the skills he should develop is the art of not playing the ball. As Marsh points out, 'Test match openers must be able to occupy the crease; this often means waiting until the threat of the new ball has been overcome before wading in with expansive cover drives.'

Marsh and Fowler are more obviously analytical than the other three and their preparation before a Test match is more calculated. Both, as soon as they learn of their selection, spend time thinking about the game in a constructive way. Says Marsh, 'I think about the bowlers I'm going to face and how they'll try to dismiss me.'

For Fowler, being a left hander, this often means an opening bowler like Imran Khan sliding the ball across his off stump, so he imagines combating that type of delivery. He regards this mental practice as being as important as any physical practice: 'After all, having a net against Graham Dilley, who swings the ball into the left hander, is not much good if I'm facing Imran Khan, who goes away from me. Obviously this mental practice has to be a positive experience; if I start thinking "I'm playing against Peter Willey, he always gets me out", I'm lost.'

This mental rehearsal is certainly not peculiar to cricket. A top class diver or gymnast, as he or she pauses before moving into action, is running the routine through his or her mind. A lot of cricketers do this automatically, while others might well benefit from such a procedure.

In the Ashes series of 1986/7 Geoff Marsh had a good idea where he expected to score his runs before going to the wicket. 'Dilley, DeFreitas and Botham bowled a lot of back foot to me (ie just short of a length), so I sweated on them bowling a bit wider so that I could cut. If they went down the leg side, I'd try to deflect for singles. Eventually, but not very often, they might give me one to drive, which is normally my strength.' This is not a particularly original plan, but the point is that Marsh knew what to expect; the absence of driveable balls was less likely to frustrate him and he was more likely to prosper as a result.

While openers do not have to endure the trauma of waiting for a wicket to fall, they have to cope with the toss of the coin. It is a time of conflicting emotions for Graeme Fowler.

'One part of me says, "I hope we bat; I'm mentally prepared; I'm ready for it", but I'd be a liar if I didn't admit to another voice saying "I hope we field; I don't want to bat against this lot (eg, the West Indies). Look how green the wicket is (it may only harbour three blades of grass) it'll be better tomorrow." As soon as I find out we're batting, I feel incredibly nervous; I have knots in my stomach. I take four deep breaths, calm down and quietly pad up. I don't like talking to people and I prefer to be left on my own.'

Marsh tends to hide himself at the back of the dressing room when the toss is being made and it's always a relief to know the outcome.

'If we're batting I have a hot shower, a cup of tea; I get my gear on and then I like to sit down and have a chat. Just before I go out I'll spend a few minutes on my own.'

It is helpful if team-mates quickly learn to appreciate the idiosyncracies of their openers so that they are sensitive towards their preferences. For instance, Mike Veletta of Western Australia needs space since he often spends the last few minutes before departure with a skipping rope to ensure that his blood is pumping and that he'll be on his toes when he arrives at the crease. I've seen others busily shadow boxing.

The five minute bell clangs and amidst cries of 'Good luck, see you at lunchtime', the two openers depart to set the tone of the innings, each time earning my silent admiration.

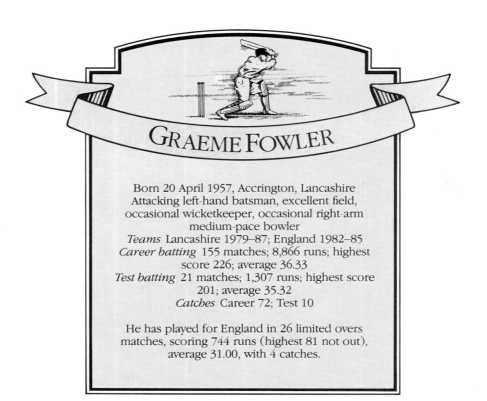

GRAEME FOWLER

Born 20 April 1957, Accrington, Lancashire
Attacking left-hand batsman, excellent field,
occasional wicketkeeper, occasional right-arm
medium-pace bowler
Teams Lancashire 1979–87; England 1982–85
Career batting 155 matches; 8,866 runs; highest
score 226; average 36.33
Test batting 21 matches; 1,307 runs; highest score
201; average 35.32
Catches Career 72; Test 10

He has played for England in 26 limited overs
matches, scoring 744 runs (highest 81 not out),
average 31.00, with 4 catches.

BUILDING AN INNINGS

No-one likes to be out first ball, particularly if it's the first ball of the match. In Tests in Australia Marsh has noticed that 'It's often the noisiest ball of the match; it's great when that happens. It gets the adrenalin flowing and you become even more determined.'

Sometimes your opponent is an unknown quantity, in which case Fowler always checks the position of the wicketkeeper to give him some idea of the bowler's pace. 'If he's more than 20 yards from the stumps, look out, because the bowler could be quick.' Once he's settled into his stance all he's thinking is 'watch the ball' and 'look to get forward'.

Every coaching book I've seen urges the batsman to watch the ball. In one of the best, *The Art of Cricket*, Bradman writes: 'The two most important pieces of advice I pass on to young batsmen are to a) concentrate and b) watch the ball. They could well be the last words before anyone goes into bat.'

However, when should you start to focus on the ball? As it's tossed from mid-off to the bowler? As the bowler starts his run? Each batsman should adopt his own routine, but Marsh doesn't zoom in on the ball until just before the bowler reaches his delivery stride for one good reason – 'It shortens my concentration span and therefore I may have more energy later in the day.' The only argument against this method is that the batsman is less likely to spot changes in the bowler's grip which might signal the inswinger or the leg cutter.

Fowler's other aim – 'look to get forward' – surprised me a little, since modern opening batsmen spend much of their time on the back foot. He explained:

'When I say "look to get forward", it doesn't mean that I'll play forward, but I've found that if I do this I move quicker. If I think about playing off the back foot against fast bowlers I find that I don't move at all; I just become lodged on my left foot. Even against the West Indies, I found that the most dangerous ball, by which I mean the most likely to dismiss me, was of a full length, so I tried to cover that one. I trusted my instincts to get me out of the way of the shorter ones.'

Indeed, any batsman who convinces himself that a bouncer is coming before the bowler has released the ball is in trouble, since he's extremely vulnerable to a full length ball if he's preparing to take evasive action.

At the start of his innings Fowler tries to leave the ball if it is outside his body width. This is a much undervalued skill. Even Viv Richards gains great satisfaction from leaving the ball alone. 'By doing that well you're exercising as much control over the bowler as if you'd played the perfect forward defensive shot. It is a very important art to master, especially if you're in poor form.'

David Gower endorses this policy when he outlines his intentions on arrival at the crease: 'I like to see the first ball;

A determined Graeme Fowler batting in Sharjah in 1983. Fowler's technique has often looked fragile and is frequently criticized, yet his Test record is most impressive. Protective headgear is noticeably absent here, although nowadays he is never seen playing without it.

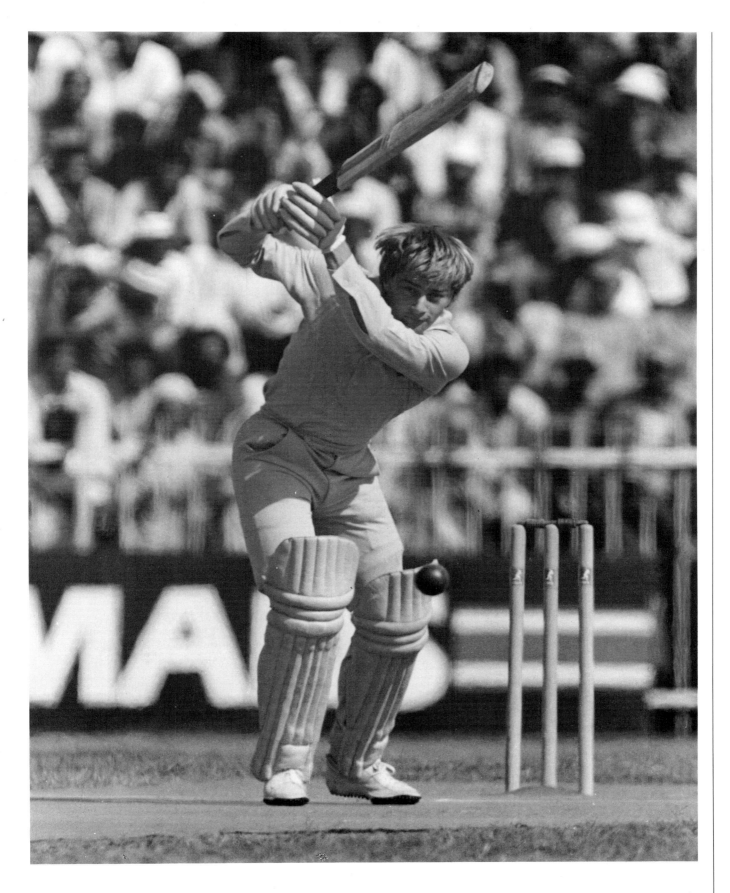

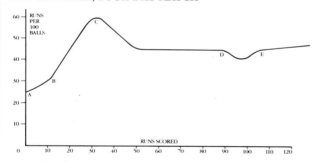

THE LIKELY RUN RATE OF A TOP CLASS PLAYER IN A TEST OR THREE/FOUR-DAY MATCH

Initially (A-B) the batsman is careful. During this period the fielding captain has probably placed a number of attacking fieldsmen in the hope of an early dismissal. Between B and C the batsman asserts his authority, maybe hitting a few boundaries through the sparsely guarded outfield so that he might move from 10 to 30 fairly rapidly. At C the fielding captain has recognized that the batsman is in control and has adjusted his field accordingly. The batsman does not expand his range of shots between C and D; in fact, if he starts to tire he may restrict himself a little. Certainly he does not take more risks as his innings progresses. The lull between D and E represents the 'nervous nineties', which afflicts some batsmen more than others.

if I don't see the first one, I like to see the second. The first 20 minutes is the time when a batsman is most vulnerable, and if I'm facing fast bowlers I try to play myself in without hitting the ball. The times I've gone in and played shots from the start, I've rarely survived long and most of my better Test knocks have been in the traditional fashion, expanding as I go along.'

The 'traditional fashion' demands that the batsman should try to play into the V between extra cover and mid-on at the start of his innings. Only when he's assessed the nature of the wicket and the bowling and also discovered his timing should he aim to drive balls or use cuts and pulls.

Such an approach has more in common with Marsh and Fowler than Botham and Richards, yet we should beware of generalizations for, as Marsh observes, 'Each innings varies; sometimes you get a couple of juicy half volleys early on and you're away; on other days the bowlers bowl well and you feel you'll never get going. But if you stick at it and stay at the crease, you know that after drinks or after lunch the runs will come.'

Of course, the likes of Botham and Richards don't always conform to the pattern shown in the graph (left).

Left *All eyes on the Don. In the pre-television era sporting heroes retained a special mystique, which is evident here from the crowd's reaction. After he retired, Bradman wrote an excellent book,* The Art of Cricket, *which is well worth reading even if you've bought a copy of this one.*

Right *Martin Crowe drives off the back foot; note the ideal position of his head. Crowe is both a perfectionist and a 'team man', a rare combination. He's capable of analyzing his own batting minutely without sacrificing his natural flair. 1st Test, England v New Zealand, Lord's, 1986.*

Botham's attitude is 'Unless I'm facing the likes of Malcolm Marshall, I'm quite happy to try to smash my first ball to the boundary if it deserves to go. I trust myself to do that. I like to dominate the bowler as soon as possible.'

Botham will adjust his game according to the circumstances, however. In the first Test of the 1986/7 Ashes series at Brisbane, Botham scored a vital century, his second 50 coming much slower than his first. Australian captain Allan Border posted half a dozen men on the boundary when Botham was on strike, tacitly admitting that he didn't expect to dismiss him and that he was therefore prepared to attack the other batsman instead. Botham sensibly resisted playing extravagant attacking shots, scored countless easy singles and sailed serenely to a century.

Botham also likes to play conservatively just before the new ball is due; this is a good example for any batsman, since the new ball often poses a fresh threat. For Botham, the attraction of meeting fire with fire is too hard to resist, and when the new ball comes out of its plastic wrapper it's the signal for a renewed assault.

Recently, Viv Richards has sometimes opted to meet 'fire with fire' at the beginning of his innings, which is contrary to the textbooks' advice but very disconcerting for a fielding captain. 'Often the bowlers look to attack me at first, so occasionally I gamble a little and make use of the open spaces. When they defend, then I may also defend more; by that time I'm usually seeing the ball well and I'm confident that I won't get out – so I consolidate, give them fewer chances.'

Like Botham, Richards wants to dominate proceedings, though maybe not in such a carefree manner; the better the bowler, the more he likes to take charge. At times he has been merciless with Underwood, who represents a genuine challenge, while he's been content to 'milk' a lesser spinner. In fact, he consciously tries to undermine his opponent's confidence. When Richards is at the crease he adopts an air of arrogance and disdain for the bowlers, which vanishes once he returns to the pavilion. He's almost like a boxer as he walks to the wicket, outstaring his adversary before the first round bell. 'If a fast bowler bowls a short one and I whack it to the boundary, I'll stroll down to the middle of the pitch and tap the wicket. I'm telling him that I'm in control and that I'm not scared of anything. Dominating a fast bowler is a joy – one of the best parts of batting.'

Above *David Gower drives Lawson off the back foot during his fine innings of 157 against Australia at The Oval in 1985 (6th Test). His feet have scarcely moved as he plays the stroke yet it is a marvellous shot.*

Below *Even the best and most experienced players suffer a few humiliating moments in the middle, so don't worry unduly if you do as well. Here Greg Chappell is embarrassed by a bouncer and is probably going to fall over.*

CONCENTRATION

We've seen how our batsmen plan their innings, but they wouldn't become centurions very often unless they had the ability to concentrate for long periods of time. Without wishing to depress you, perhaps I should remind you that the fitter you are the longer you can concentrate. Players adopt a variety of routines to help them. Derek Randall talks to himself loudly – 'Come on, Rags, come on'. Chris Tavaré goes for a ponderous perambulation towards square leg to gather his thoughts. Sunil Gavaskar often uses his hands as blinkers between balls to shut out any distractions. Ian Botham sometimes talks to himself and has been known to chat to close fielders as well while the bowler runs in. Meanwhile, Geoff Boycott appears completely and utterly relaxed at the crease as if it's his natural habitat.

Most batsmen like to chat to one another between overs as this reduces the feeling of loneliness out there and makes the wicket a slightly more comfortable place to be, even if you're out of form. These conversations are usually pretty desultory rather than the stuff of high drama – something like, 'well played; keep working; he's stopped swinging it; square leg has moved deeper'. In other words, encouragement and a few technical observations. Occasionally, these conversations might broaden to 'there's a frightfully good-looking lady at deep backward square-leg', or a sudden flash of inspiration will solve the crossword clue that you had both been puzzling over an hour before. Anything is better than a feeling of wretched isolation.

Often the setting of short term targets helps – another 20 minutes or the lunch interval. Brearley recalls how he and Randall in the Centenary Test at Melbourne decided to separate the afternoon session into 15-minute segments, which prompted the enthusiastic Randall to say, 'Stick at it, skip, in another 10 minutes, it'll be 15 minutes to tea.' A young Geoff Marsh was once opening the batting with Ric Charlesworth for Western Australia against Queensland; they were playing well and they set themselves a target of a 150 partnership. Once this was achieved, Marsh was dismissed immediately and semi-seriously blamed the more experienced Charlesworth for not setting a fresh target.

When concentrating properly a batsman should be in complete charge of his body and mind. Peter Roebuck, Somerset's opener, is one of the most controlled and

FORCING SHOT OFF THE BACK FOOT

Also called a back foot drive, this shot is played to a ball that is short of a length and too straight to cut. It is often favoured by taller players. Shorter players tend to be more adept at cutting.

Right The backlift is high. As the body turns the back foot is back and across to allow space for the stroke.

Far right A good high finish, with the bat pointing in the direction of the hit and the batsman coming onto his toes to use his height as he strikes through the ball.

AVOIDING ACTION

Against short pitched bowling you have four choices: a defensive shot, a hook, ducking and swaying. Whichever you choose, try to keep your eye on the ball.

Far left A good ducking position, with the batsman still looking at the ball and keeping his bat out of harm's way.

Left Swaying to the leg side to allow a high, rising ball to pass harmlessly over the stumps. The bat is lowered.

clinical of English batsmen. Nonetheless, he admits to occasional uncontrollable urges to smash the next ball over the bowler's head. Yet even Botham stresses the importance of not premeditating the shots he would like to play during a long innings. It's all very well itching to play your favourite cover drive, but if the ball is pitched short of a length on leg stump, it's clearly impossible. One ball at a time and no preconceived ideas.

Playing and missing can also undermine a batsman's concentration disastrously. When Marsh plays and misses, he says, 'I walk away and quickly analyze why I missed it. Maybe the ball was too wide or I was lazy; maybe it was a really good ball. Then I forget about it and switch on to the next one. There's nothing to be gained from worrying about your form or your technique while in the middle.' Indeed, there's something demoralizing for a bowler when he sees a batsman who is totally unconcerned about being beaten. The theatrical glee of a bowler who has just won a moral victory is usually calculated to undermine the confidence of the batsman; yet indifference to this defeat can also deflate the bowler.

Another danger period is after the fall of a wicket. After a long partnership, the two successful batsmen often return to the pavilion within the space of 10 minutes. Fowler is always aware of this possibility and consciously tightens up his technique and restricts his stroke-play until his new partner is settled. An extreme example of this occurred in the Perth Test of 1982/3. Chris Tavaré, having batted steadily for the first $4\frac{1}{2}$ hours of the match, witnessed the fall of two quick wickets. As a result, he failed to score during the last $1\frac{1}{2}$ hours of play. This was a typically selfless piece of batting as he attempted to adjust to the team's needs and protect his wicket at all costs, though whether the end result in this case served the best interests of the team is debatable.

For 90 per cent of the time, captains and fast bowlers, anxious for a rest in the pavilion, enjoy having so-called 'selfish' batsmen in their team, especially if we regard 'selfish' as meaning that the batsman treasures his wicket at all times. It pays to be greedy. If a player survives the first 20 minutes when he is most vulnerable, he should, as Ken Barrington once said, 'book in for bed and breakfast', since there will be plenty of occasions when those first 20 minutes prove fatal. Captains and coaches have more reason to be frustrated by batsmen who are consistently dismissed for 20 or 30 rather than 0 or 1.

Fowler amused, Kirmani pensive and Kapil bored. Fowler enjoyed a successful series in India in 1984 and showed that nimble footwork is invaluable against spin as well as pace. He scored a superb double century in Madras where he worked out a pattern of play against the Indian spinners and assiduously stuck to it for eight hours.

THE BIG OCCASION

What has separated Viv Richards from many other great cricketers of this era has been his consistent ability to succeed on the big occasion. At Lord's, in five one-day finals for Somerset and three World Cup finals for the West Indies, he failed just once, way back in 1975. On many occasions he has produced match-winning centuries. I asked him how he has managed to sustain this remarkable record over the years.

'Some players, when their side has reached a final, relax a little; the occasion takes over and they are content simply to be a part of it. I'm not so naïve; I need results. In a final, there's a big audience and I want to be remembered. Too many good players flake out on the big occasion.

'This happened to me in my first final with Somerset in 1978. [Somerset lost to Sussex in the Gillette Cup;

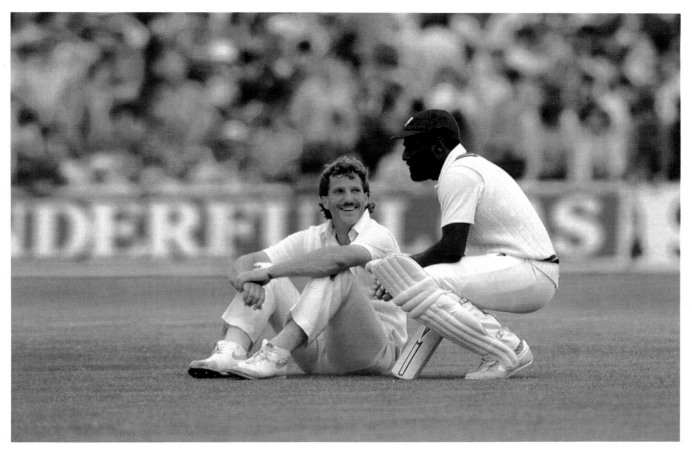

Richards and Botham in opposition. Chatting and joking often help rather than hinder a batsman, enabling the player to relax before reaching a peak of concentration for about 10–15 seconds while the ball is bowled and played. Former Somerset all rounder Bill Alley was often 'sent to Coventry' by opponents since he was only happy if he was talking.

Richards scored a tenative 40, which would have been quite acceptable to most of us, but not him.] *I thought I had to look different. I made sure that I was wearing a new pair of lily-white flannels and that my bat was reasonably new rather than using the gear that I'd had during the rest of that season. By doing that, I was changing my character and betraying my nervousness; the occasion had taken over.*

'The next time I stuck to my normal routine and I decided to dominate the event. I tried to be as calm and controlled as possible, forgetting that this was the final, even though the adrenalin was flowing a little faster than usual. Also, I'll admit that I like showing off and a final at Lord's is the best possible platform. In addition I recognized that maybe half the side was not in such a positive frame of mind, therefore it was my responsibility to succeed and not put any pressure on the others. When I was batting, I wanted to make sure that no-one else was going to come in. It was my stage.'

Few of us can ever hope to dominate a match in the same way that Richards can, but maybe we can learn from his approach. Daryl Foster, who has prepared several Western Australia sides for Sheffield Shield finals, endorses what Richards says.

'As far as possible I like my players to stick to the same routine before a big match. Sudden bursts of Churchillian oratory or a string of motivational videos can arouse a player to a degree that can affect him detrimentally. Each player has a different optimum level of arousal and a coach must be sensitive to this.'

When I first entered an England dressing room, I was amazed by the levity of the atmosphere. I can recall in particular John Lever of Essex being very funny, not because he had a blasé attitude towards the game; it was simply his way of reducing the tension, something that most of us yearned for.

Foster is adamant that a coach should never concentrate upon the mistakes that might occur. 'That produces a negative environment since the only time a coach says anything is when a player is doing something wrong. He should emphasize the positive aspects of the performances of a team or a player. Fear of failure is the most destructive element in sport and the coach – and, indeed, the captain – should aim to reduce that anxiety.

'What have I done?' Ian Botham after his astonishing 145 not out against the Australians during the 3rd Test at Headingley in 1981. In the previous Test he'd scored a 'pair' and was relieved as England's captain; his career had rarely looked bleaker. Three hours of unbridled strokeplay at Headingley changed that and found him back in his winning ways.

In times of stress, it often helps to cut yourself off from the performance of the rest of the team and not to worry about the end result. Each player should just concentrate on that particular area of the game where he is expected to contribute, in the knowledge that if everyone manages to do this, the whole team's performance should prove satisfactory at 6.30 pm.

COMBATING DIFFERENT TYPES OF BOWLING

The following section is not intended to be comprehensive; it merely gives a few examples of how different players combat different types of bowling. Every batsman needs to work out his own method of survival and run-scoring. Against fast bowling, some will hook, some will sway and others will duck identical balls; against spinners, some will advance down the wicket to execute ferocious straight drives, while others will scamper ones and twos. Each individual has to assess his own strengths and weaknesses and bat accordingly.

For the likes of Richards and Botham these limitations often appear to be negligible, whereas for Marks and others, who had better remain nameless, they are more obvious. Yet there have been a few occasions when Marks has outscored Richards in a day's play!

Pace

Len Hutton is supposed to have observed that the best way to play fast bowling is 'from the other end'. There is a certain unarguable logic behind this statement, but it is not quite sufficient.

When I asked my five batsmen whether they changed their technique significantly when they were facing Malcolm Marshall rather than Richard Ellison's away swingers, I half expected them to outline massive adjustments. They didn't. However, some players have completely remodelled their technique in an attempt to combat the short rising delivery that has become so commonplace over the last 15 years. For instance, Alan Knott began a minor revolution in Kent. Against fast bowling, he changed his grip so that his top hand was behind the handle of the bat, thus enabling him to put his hands in front of his face while keeping the bat straight.

This improvisation influenced several of the other Kent players such as Bob Woolmer and Chris Tavaré, both extremely gifted batsmen, but I have often wondered whether such a radical change in technique didn't restrict the likes of Tavaré when batting against anything other than extreme pace. Certainly, for players in club cricket, I would be wary of advocating a change of grip to combat one particular type of bowling, which would be confronted fairly infrequently.

While Fowler and Marsh don't alter their technique against pace bowlers, they might amend the areas in which they expect to score. For example, against Marshall, Fowler would be more wary of cutting since, he says, 'He makes the ball bounce a lot and he's so quick that you have to be absolutely precise in your bat movement; there is no margin for error. Against Richard Ellison you have time to adjust to the bounce, simply because the ball is travelling

Gordon Greenidge drives with a full swing of the bat during his 223 against England at Old Trafford in 1984. If you ever get the opportunity to watch Greenidge, note especially his footwork; it is both precise and decisive. When he plays back, his right foot is just inches from the stumps; when forward, he's often positioned 3ft in front of the crease.

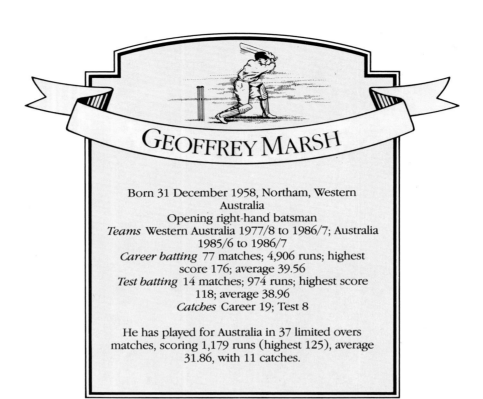

GEOFFREY MARSH

Born 31 December 1958, Northam, Western
Australia
Opening right-hand batsman
Teams Western Australia 1977/8 to 1986/7; Australia
1985/6 to 1986/7
Career batting 77 matches; 4,906 runs; highest
score 176; average 39.56
Test batting 14 matches; 974 runs; highest score
118; average 38.96
Catches Career 19; Test 8

He has played for Australia in 37 limited overs
matches, scoring 1,179 runs (highest 125), average
31.86, with 11 catches.

slower.' However, the speed of the ball makes leg side deflections more profitable, and Marsh can find one consolation: 'Because the express bowlers tend to have an array of slips, if you manage to get the full face of the bat to the ball you can pick up ones and twos through mid-off; a slower bowler usually has this area covered.'

Fowler and Marsh rarely attempt to hook short pitched balls, but Gower is less predictable. He says, 'It's not a great idea to hook too early in an innings when playing the West Indians. However, when I do look to hook, I often find that I watch the ball better. If I can get into the right position for the shot, I can usually get out of the way.' Gower doesn't lay down strict rules for himself: 'I've hooked them all, I've ducked them all and I've been hit on the head by some of them.' This is probably the wisest approach. Kim Hughes, during his final, ill-fated season as Australia's captain, declared not only to the dressing room, but also to the Australian public, that he was promptly going to stop hooking in all circumstances, but in his next innings the inevitable happened...

As I've already mentioned, Richards and Botham are not keen on imposing limitations on themselves, yet both admit to loitering on the back foot a little longer against extreme pace. They may have been totally carefree in the Seventies, but they are more worldly wise now. In 1974 there were some titanic battles between the two young Antiguan colleagues, Richards and Roberts, when they met in Somerset/Hampshire games. If Roberts bowled a bouncer, it was a matter of pride for Richards to deposit the ball into the old organ works at Taunton. Nowadays he allows more deliveries to fly harmlessly over his head.

Swing

When the ball is new, it is most likely to swing, or 'hoop', as they say in Australia. Fowler tries to play the ball with the swing, so if he is facing Ellison, who predominantly swings the ball into him, he aims to play good length balls towards mid-on rather than the covers. Imran usually swings the ball away from the left hander in pursuit of catches in the slip cordon, so Fowler aims to get right behind the ball and either leave it or play towards mid-off.

Against swing bowlers, it is doubly important to watch the ball on to the bat and to 'play late', by which I mean not lunging forward and playing the first line of the ball, but adjusting as it swings through the air. If the ball is swinging away consistently Marsh consciously plays outside the line of the ball when playing a forward defensive shot. 'Against Dilley and Hadlee I used my front pad quite frequently,' he says. This method naturally reduces the chances of an outside edge, while marginally increasing the possibility of being LBW. In Australia, however, I have observed that if you play forward and straight the chances of being given LBW are relatively small, while in England umpires are generally a little less reluctant to give LBWs on the front foot. The reason for this may be because the ball doesn't usually bounce as high on English grounds as it does on Australian ones.

A controlled square cut by Geoff Marsh; 3rd Test, Australia v England, Adelaide, 1986. Like Bill Lawry and Bobby Simpson before him, Marsh curbed his aggressive instincts when selected to open for his country, sacrificing a few shots for the sake of consistency. Each batsman must find out for himself the most effective balance.

Spin

The philosophy of Richards and Botham against spinners is straightforward and familiar. They intend always to dominate them. Richards says, 'Certain bowlers, given the chance, can create havoc. For instance, Derek Underwood is so accurate and frustrating that he can bowl with men around the bat all day unless you take the initiative, so throughout my career I've always adopted an aggressive approach against him. Also, I know that he hates to be hit. In fact, I came to be able to predict how he would react when I was attacking him – when he would bowl his quicker ball or his slower flighted delivery. So I make it my first aim to scatter the close fielders in front of the bat.'

I actually think that it can be regarded as a compliment to a spinner if Richards launches a full blooded assault against him, since he has often adopted the same policy against John Emburey, whom he regards as an excellent bowler. Once the close fielders have evaporated into the middle distance Richards is usually content to 'milk' them by picking up plenty of singles, interspersed with the occasional boundary. Botham combats spinners in a similar way, though he is more likely to disregard completely the presence of a long off since he's so confident that he can clear him.

Sunil Gavaskar square cuts while David Bairstow looks on. Gavaskar has scored more Test centuries than any other batsman, thanks to a superb technique combined with an extraordinary capacity to concentrate for long periods of time. 4th Test, England v India, The Oval, 1979.

Of course, Richards and Botham do not represent the norm; most players are less capable and less prepared to risk a full assault. Indeed, Geoff Marsh is unworried by having men clustered around the bat since he reasons that their presence means there are more gaps elsewhere and therefore more opportunities for run-scoring. The glaring presence of close fielders also sharpens his concentration – 'They make me more determined.'

However, if the silly-point and short-leg remain in position, it is essential that more care should be taken when playing defensive shots, since the batsman cannot afford to allow the ball to pop up off the inside edge and the pad. Marsh says, 'I always ensure that my hands are very soft and relaxed on the bat. I won't push at the ball, but I'll let the ball hit the bat gently so that it dies straightaway. If the ball isn't turning, I try to use my bat all the time, but if an off spinner is deviating the ball, I usually play with my bat behind my front pad.' This often results in the ball striking

THE CUT

The square cut is played to a short of a length ball a foot or more outside the off stump. Gordon Greenidge plays this shot superbly. The illustrations below show the square cut (left and middle) and the late cut (right). For a good example of the finish of the square cut, see the photograph of Geoff Marsh on p. 53.

The leading shoulder has turned and the weight is on the back foot.

The arms hit downwards at full stretch.

For the late cut the ball is struck when the bat is level with the stumps.

THE HOOK

The hook can be played to a short, fast delivery that rises to shoulder height. Before an innings a batsman should know how he intends to react to such deliveries.

The finish of the hook – the body pivots with the batsman looking to hook down.

DEFENSIVE SHOTS

For most players, straight, good length balls require defensive shots, especially at the start of an innings. The artworks below show the forward defence (left and middle) and the back defence (right).

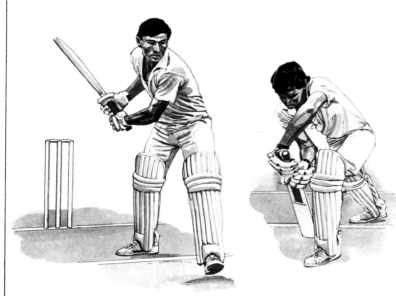

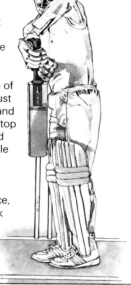

Far left The head and front shoulder lead with the front leg moving towards and bending into the pitch of the ball.

Left The head is on the line of the ball, which is pitching just outside off stump. The bat and pad are close together. The top hand controls the stroke and holds the bat at a slight angle to direct the ball down.

Right A good sideways position for the back defence, with the weight on the back foot. The top hand is in control, as for the forward defensive, and the bottom hand is relaxed.

the front pad but, because the bat is in close proximity to it, it is deemed to be playing a shot and is therefore unlikely to produce LBWs. Being an off spinner myself, I find this method of batting extremely frustrating to counter, but I admit that it's very effective.

Against a spinner who has good control, it helps to have a clear idea of where you intend to score your runs. David Gower likes hitting off spinners through the off side; as a result, most off spinners try to bowl a tight line to him. Depending on the situation of the game, Gower says, 'I either remain patient and wait for him to give me some room or I'll use my feet to drive through extra cover or straight over the top. Sometimes these shots are premeditated, but not always; there are times when I just react when the ball is tossed a little higher.'

It is only against spinners that premeditated shots have any chance of regular success. Botham explains, 'Sometimes, I set myself up for a lofted drive, but now I have the presence of mind to press the safety valve and adjust if the ball is not in the right place.' Geoff Marsh doesn't premeditate individual shots, but he may decide on an overall plan of attack when a slow bowler begins a spell. For instance, if an off spinner is bowling to him without a deep mid-wicket he may decide that, if the bowler bowls the ball on a full length at middle/leg stump, he will hit it in the air to the deep mid-wicket boundary. If he succeeds a

couple of times, this poses problems for the bowler since he is bound to plug that shot, thereby creating gaps in the field elsewhere.

Finally, let me give one example from my own experience of how a player can formulate a plan against a particular bowler. It concerns my attempts to play against Abdul Qadir in Pakistan in 1983. It should not be taken as the way to play leg spin bowling but, given my own considerable limitations as a batsman, it demonstrates how a preconceived plan can help neutralize the effect of such a formidable opponent.

In two consecutive innings I had been utterly bemused by Qadir's wrist spin. Not only could I not predict which way the ball would bounce, but I had enormous difficulties judging where it would bounce. Such is Qadir's skill as a spinner that he is capable of making the ball dip at the end of its flight, so that what appeared to me to be juicy half volleys ended up as good length balls which had me groping like a blind man.

Fortunately, the next two matches were played on slow, flat wickets and I hit upon a system that worked – at least temporarily – for me. I decided that under no circumstances would I attempt to drive him, since I was unable to judge his flight. Nor would I lunge at him, since that would probably produce bat/pad catches close to the wicket; so I blocked half volleys on the front foot and, since the pitches

Two superb examples of defensive shots from two contrasting players, Richards (above) and Boycott (below right). The position of their heads and left elbows should send the most demanding coach into ecstasy. When Richards plays defensively bowlers sometimes feel that he is toying with them; not so with Boycott. Boycott's forward defensive is against an Indian spinner (at Edgbaston, 1979): notice how the bat is just behind the pad so that if he edges the ball, which looks unlikely, it will fall to the ground rather than pop up off the pad straight to a short-leg fieldsman.

were so slow, I was able to play good length balls off the back foot. I assumed that balls pitching outside the off stump were googlies and those on the stumps, leg breaks. Scoring shots were restricted to the cut, the occasional pull and the sweep if the ball was outside leg stump. It was not a pretty sight for the spectators but it worked for a while. Gradually I could sense some frustration on his part when he hadn't dismissed me after half an hour, for it was up to him to take the initiative away and change the established pattern by bowling around the wicket or shuffling his fielders. Obviously, more able players had other options and played him differently; but one of the arts of batting, which can't be stated too often so I'll stress it again, is to learn to be aware of one's limitations and strengths and then to bat accordingly.

THE SWEEP

The sweep is usually played to a ball of good length
pitching outside leg stump (unless you're Alan Knott).

The head and shoulder lead to
bring the pad onto the line of
the ball.

The knee of the back leg bends.
The arms are at full stretch
as they bring the bat down.

A good finish, with the head
over the front knee and not
turning away too early.

RUNNING BETWEEN THE WICKETS

Two fleet-footed batsmen scurrying between the wickets
can sometimes change the course of a game as effectively
as the mighty hitter. The glorious off-drive to a long-off
fieldsman, followed by a leisurely trot to the other end, is
worth no more than an inside nick on to the pads which
drops 3 feet from the wicket and easily results in one run to
the batsman's name. While the advent of so much limited
overs cricket has undoubtedly improved the general
standard of fielding, it has also sharpened batsmen's
awareness of the importance of alert running between the
wickets.

Conversely, there's nothing worse for the morale of a
batting side than to see a needless run out through
misjudgement or indecision. One of the most ominous
experiences in cricket is to hear the words 'Hurry up' as
you pass your partner. It's surprising that two of the most
accomplished post-war English batsmen of contrasting
styles, namely Compton and Boycott, gained reputations
as poor runners. It is now cricketing folklore, whether true
or not, that Compton's first call could only be used as a
basis for negotiation.

Since the same well-tried rules should apply whether it's
a Test match or a beer match, I've decided to adopt a
schoolmasterly tone for a while.

Calls should be made swiftly and loudly – 'Yes', 'No',
'Wait'. Try to avoid one of my colleagues' favourite calls,
which is 'Go'; on a windy day this has caused desperate
confusion. The striker is responsible for calling when the
ball is hit in front of the wicket while the non striker calls
for strokes behind the wicket, but each player should be
prepared to contradict his partner's call if he spots danger.
This should be done without delay.

Once the ball has been delivered, the non striker should
back up so that he is 3 or 4 yards down the wicket when the
shot is played.

When taking a sharp single it's important to slide the bat
into the crease, as this is the quickest way of getting there.

Unless there's obviously no chance of a second run,
follow the well-worn maxim of 'running the first one
quickly'. If you do this a fumble by third man or long-leg
can easily produce an extra run as well as scowls from the
bowler and fielding captain.

When contemplating a second or third run, don't 'turn
blind' – ie, always turn towards that side of the ground to
which the ball has been struck. This allows you to judge
the possibility of an extra run much more quickly. Surprisingly many first class cricketers fail to master this skill. Also,
when crossing, give your partner an idea whether another
run is possible.

It is valuable to build up a knowledge of your opponents; which fielders are left handed, which have strong
arms, who is quick and not so quick. Arthur Francis, once

Above *Allan Border is not the most stylish batsman in the world, but he is one of the most effective. Here he is seen executing an orthodox sweep shot. Note the limited follow through of the bat; it is important to remember that to try to hit the sweep shot too hard is a mistake. Some players, like Alan Knott, drove slow bowlers to distraction by sweeping balls that were straight or pitching outside off stump. For Knott, length rather than line determined whether or not he would attempt to play the shot. 3rd Test, Australia v England, Adelaide, 1986.*

Right *The unorthodox or reverse sweep displayed by Ian Botham against New Zealand at Trent Bridge, 1983. This shot must be premeditated since it requires a right handed batsman to change his grip to that of a left hander. It is a delight to watch and, no doubt, very satisfying to play. Certainly it upsets off spinners. In English County cricket, apart from Botham, Derek Pringle and Derek Randall play this very risky shot well, usually against off spinners bowling to a leg side field during limited overs matches. Peter May never played it.*

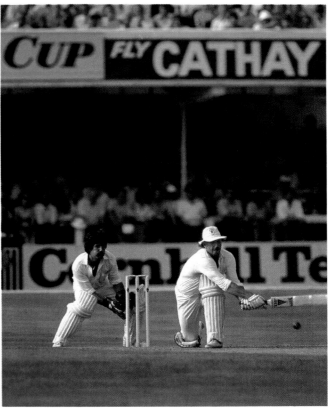

of Glamorgan, probably didn't make a huge impact on the County scene in the late Seventies and early Eighties except that a few batsmen discovered, rather too late, that he was ambidextrous. A County side playing at Hove in recent years has learnt not to take any liberties when the ball is near Paul Parker, one of the finest outfielders of the last decade. Conversely, don't be afraid to exploit more ponderous fielders, who shall remain nameless.

Remember, too, that you have a responsibility for your partner's safety as well as your own. You may have the

THE PULL

The pull is played against a short ball or long hop, which is too close to the body for the batsman to cut. Don Bradman, when glimpsed on film, always seems to be pulling.

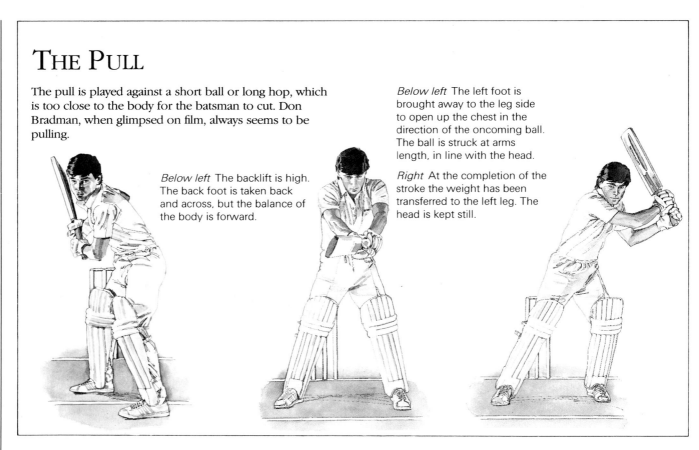

Below left The backlift is high. The back foot is taken back and across, but the balance of the body is forward.

Below left The left foot is brought away to the leg side to open up the chest in the direction of the oncoming ball. The ball is struck at arms length, in line with the head.

Right At the completion of the stroke the weight has been transferred to the left leg. The head is kept still.

speed of an Olympic sprinter, but your partner may not be similarly blessed.

If you bat regularly with the same partner you may well build up a sort of telepathic understanding and calling might become unnecessary; a look or a nod is sufficient. Apparently Hobbs and Sutcliffe stole singles without a sound; on a slightly less exalted plane, Brian Rose and Peter Denning did the same for Somerset in the late Seventies. This can be most disconcerting for a fielding side, who are robbed of any audible sign that the batsmen are running. However, it's dangerous to try this with unfamiliar partners.

During a partnership, the batsmen should discuss the position of the in-field. For instance, cover and mid-wicket might be hanging back, mindful of saving fours – in which case a few quick singles will bring them closer, improving your chances of reaching the boundary. Moreover, bowlers of every ilk detest seeing a perfectly good delivery yielding one run from a nondescript shot.

Of course, even if you obey the rules, the odd fiasco will occur. If you, the lesser player, find yourself stranded mid-wicket staring at the side's star batsman from a distance of 2 feet, then the proper thing to do is to sacrifice your wicket rather than his. This is obviously disappointing but it permits you to play the martyr for a while (providing the initial misunderstanding wasn't totally your fault) and it should earn you plenty of drinks later that evening.

LIMITED OVERS

Peter Roebuck was once asked how he changed his game in limited over matches. 'I try to hit it further and more often,' was his response. Need I go on?

The players I interviewed, all being early order batsmen and among the best players in their respective sides, stressed that they tried to change their game as little as possible. They reckoned, quite reasonably, that if they stayed in and batted normally, they would score runs quickly enough for the team's requirements. The most significant difference they noted was that they played at more wide balls than in first class cricket, often opening the face of the bat to guide the ball down to third man for a single.

Viv Richards thinks that his batting has suffered from one-day cricket. Like many English County players, he gets 'that Monday morning feeling'. 'On Mondays (after Sunday's 40-over match), I often start batting as if it were a Sunday League match when there are no slips and I play at everything.' Yet the one-day game has provoked some of Richards' finest innings; his 189 not out against England at Old Trafford in 1984 could not have been surpassed by anyone. It was a day when 'everything clicked: I could have scored 200 but I had to try to keep the strike by taking singles!'

On the credit side, the one-day games can act as a

Above *He who hesitates is lost. England's Wilf Slack has just applied the brakes but too late to prevent Joel Garner from swooping on the ball and running him out. Such a dismissal is the most frustrating and wasteful in cricket. Unfortunately, it's happened to most of us at some time or another. 2nd Test, Trinidad, 1986.*

Right *Richards acknowledges the applause of the crowd – and the England team – on his superlative innings of 189 not out. The tradition of applauding an opponent still survives in top class cricket, happily. It's hard to imagine a full back congratulating the opposition's winger on scoring a superb goal in a Football League game.*

catalyst for some players. They discover a new range of shots and hitherto uncharted talents. Limited overs cricket certainly aided Glenn Turner's transformation as a batsman.

David Gower is always urged by his Leicestershire colleagues 'just to bat for 30 overs' since he's a natural striker of the ball; after that he is permitted a few liberties, but Gower has learnt that 'I can hit the ball to the boundary far more easily without slogging: I rely on timing rather than brute strength, so I'll never wind up like a blacksmith to smash the ball'.

Similarly Geoff Marsh, despite being a farmer's son, rarely plays any agricultural shots. 'Obviously I try to hit boundaries, but I've found when opening with David Boon for Australia that he's more likely to hit boundaries than I am; so if it's one of his days I'm content to pick up singles.

IAN BOTHAM

Born 24 November 1955, Heswall, Cheshire
Attacking middle-order right-hand batsman, right-arm fast-medium bowler, excellent close field
Teams Somerset 1974–86; Worcestershire 1987; England 1977–86/7
Career batting 298 matches; 15,160 runs; highest score 228; average 35.33
Career bowling 298 matches; 954 wickets; best bowling 8–34; average 26.38
Test batting 89 matches; 4,825 runs: highest score 208; average 34.96
Test bowling 89 matches; 366 wickets; best bowling 8–34; average 27.21
Catches Career 271; Test 106

He is the world's leading Test all rounder, being the first player to achieve the 'double' of 3,000 runs and 300 wickets. His century to win the Headingley Ashes Test of 1981 is legendary. He captained England in 12 Tests in 1980 and 1981. In 92 limited overs matches for England he has scored 1,663 runs (highest 72), average 22.78, with 30 catches; and has taken 116 wickets (best 4–56), average 28.40. He left Somerset in 1986 in sympathy with Richards and Garner, and joined Worcestershire in 1987.

Watching Geoff Boycott in 1979 in the one-day series in Australia has always stuck in my mind; he played superbly that year, but most of his runs were from singles or twos rather than boundaries; very often the side that scores the most singles wins the game.'

So you don't have to be an explosive hitter to be successful in limited overs cricket. In England, Clive Radley of Middlesex, who is affectionately known as 'the run thief' on the County circuit, has demonstrated this time and time again. He probably hits a couple of sixes a year. However, he's a superb judge of a run, a clever improviser and he scores off a remarkably high proportion of balls faced. Amazingly, he is still doing that at the age of 43.

Towards the end of an innings, batsmen in pursuit of boundaries have started to move around like ballroom dancers as the bowler reaches the wicket. Usually they are trying to combat a bowler who is firing the ball at leg stump; the batsman moves away to the leg side so that he has enough room to swing the bat effectively. However, such a ploy is obviously risky and often over-used. If your head is constantly on the move as the bowler delivers it is much harder to hit the ball which, after all, is the main aim. Also, by moving away from the line of the ball you are far more likely to be yorked by experienced bowlers. However, that gap at deep extra cover is often very tempting and can be irresistible.

Inevitably, Richards is one of the best exponents of this ploy. He makes a special effort to keep his head still. Moreover, although the movement is premeditated, he doesn't necessarily aim to hit the ball to one pre-ordained part of the ground. 'If the bowler keeps his normal line I'll aim for the extra cover boundary, but if he follows me as I move away, then I'm still looking for the "pick up" over square leg.'

Richards has the eye to do this successfully, but for normal players I think the best approach is to watch the ball, aim to hit straight and run like the wind. Up until the last over there's no point in sacrificing your wicket by playing shots with a 20 per cent success rate. As all County captains say to their batsmen when they are contemplating a run chase, 'Wickets in hand are crucial'.

Botham alert and ready to strike. Technically, he is in an excellent position. The backlift is generous and straight. The head is still and perfectly poised with eyes level and watching the oncoming ball. Even the most exciting and extravagant of players base their game on a sound technique.

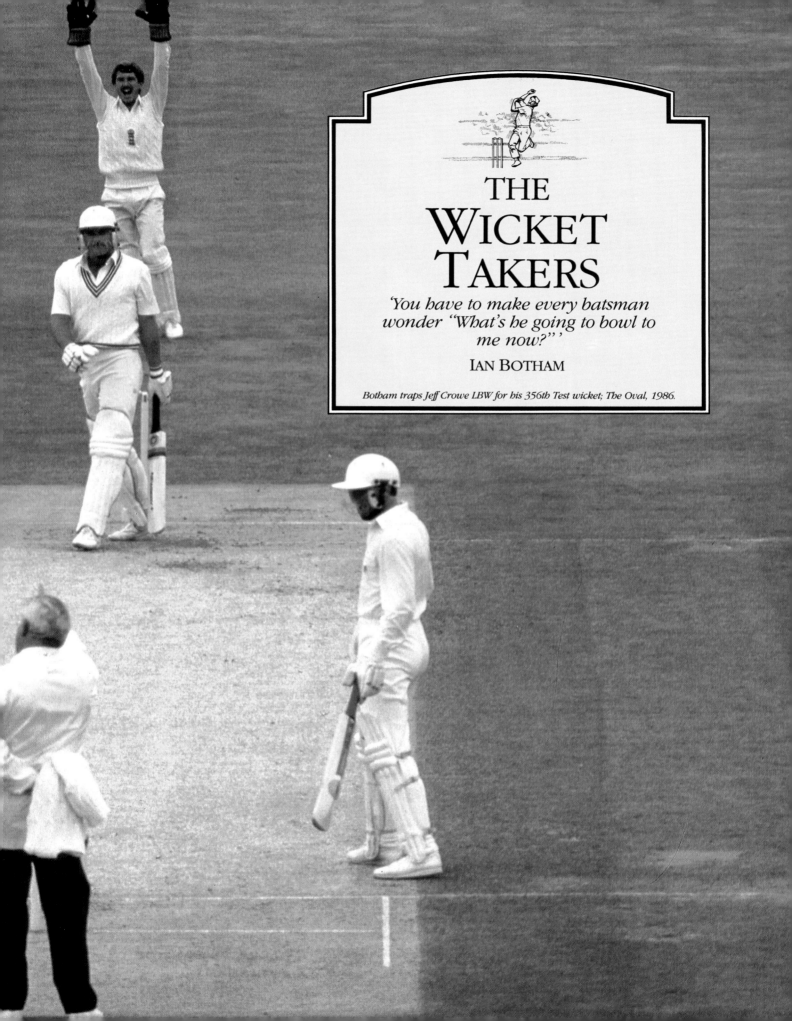

THE
WICKET
TAKERS

'You have to make every batsman wonder "What's he going to bowl to me now?"'

IAN BOTHAM

Botham traps Jeff Crowe LBW for his 356th Test wicket; The Oval, 1986.

*B*owlers win matches; batsmen save them. In English County Cricket 90 per cent of the overseas players, all of whom are enlisted in the hope of transforming an average side into a Championship winning one, are bowlers – most of them fast. Yet bowlers have often been regarded as the workhorses of cricket. The batsmen get the glory, the bowlers blisters. Maybe this is a hangover from Victorian times. Ranji informs us that 'practically all bowling in county matches is done by professionals and the average professional is much superior to the average amateur bowler ... When a bowler chosen to play for the Gentlemen cannot accept the invitation, it is generally very difficult to fill his place. With the Players the difficulty is whom not to include.' Bowling was deemed to be rather hard work for amateurs.

Every young cricketer should discover whether he can bowl, if only to punctuate those long sessions in the field as well as increase his chances of selection. Andrew Kennedy at Taunton School sees a lot of 10 and 11-year-olds in the nets and is anxious not to categorize them as fast/slow or spin/seam too early in their careers. 'To begin with I'll just watch from a distance; some are obviously naturals, whether spin or speed, so I leave them; others look wrong, so I gently encourage them to experiment with different styles. If there's no sign of progress in any of them, it might be time to get the wicketkeeping gloves out. Every young cricketer should strive to develop more than one facet of the game.'

The advent of so much limited overs cricket has not altered the bowler's main aim, which is to dismiss the batsman. There are five types of dismissal that can be accredited to the bowler: bowled, caught, LBW, stumped and hit the wicket. (The four other modes of dismissal can result from a batsman's self-destructive streak. Easily the most frequent of these is 'run out'. The others are 'handled the ball', 'hit the ball twice' and 'obstructing the field', but these methods have accounted for only 61 dismissals in the history of first class cricket.)

BOWLING BASICS

These diagrams demonstrate the basic action which any beginner should seek to emulate. The grip shown is for a seam bowler.

Don't worry if you don't fulfil all the criteria – Procter, Garner, Willis and Thomson didn't either.

Left The ball is held between the first two fingers and the thumb. The fingers are placed either side of the seam, which is upright, while the thumb and third finger support the ball.

Right The body is turning sideways. The front shoulder will point down the pitch. The bowler's landing foot (right) is also turning to land parallel to the crease.

Above right The body is now sideways to the batsman with the head looking from behind the front arm. The front knee is raised and the body is leaning away from the batsman.

While all bowlers have the same goal, they often achieve it in vastly differing ways. First class cricket has accommodated bowlers of all shapes and sizes. Joel Garner and Clarrie Grimmett have very similar Test records yet their method of bowling and their physique have absolutely nothing in common. Batsmen can be undermined by giants and midgets, by sheer speed, by swing and by spin and flight. A well-balanced bowling attack will have a sprinkling of all types so that it may adapt to the prevailing conditions.

Bowlers vary not only in their physical attributes but also in their mental approach. Some are cunning, patient and distant; they frustrate their opponents and force them into error through relentless accuracy (like Emburey or Cartwright). Others are brimful of aggression and hostility and expect to take a wicket with each ball they bowl; these are the characteristics of many of the great fast bowlers (for example Trueman and Lillee). It is with pace bowling that we shall start.

Richard Hadlee's smooth, rhythmical run up and action provide the perfect model for any aspiring fast bowler. Unusually, he was more devastating at 35 than at 25.

The front leg is straightening as the ball is released from a high front arm.

The head is still looking at the batsman as the arm extends back. The right leg has been brought through close to the left leg.

The head is looking along the leading shoulder. The stride length is important for establishing a firm base.

FAST BOWLER TO A RIGHT-HAND BATSMAN
This diagram shows an aggressive field which a fast bowler might employ at the start of a three/five-day game. Notice that there are three slips and a gully awaiting an outside edge. If the batsman is tentative, 9 might reinforce the slip cordon or move to backward short-leg.

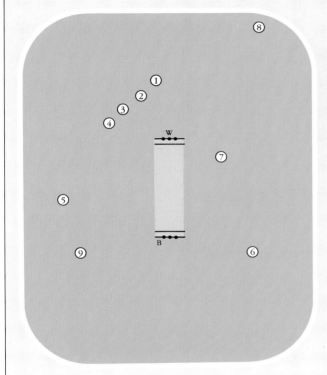

Key: 1, first slip; 2, second slip; 3, third slip; 4, gully; 5, cover point; 6, mid-on; 7, forward short-leg; 8, long leg; 9, mid-off.

THE PACE BOWLER

Pace bowlers have undoubtedly decided more Test series than any other type of cricketer. They have also captured the public's imagination more and have become synonymous with certain series – Larwood in 1932/3, Tyson in 1954/5, Snow in 1970/1, Lillee and Thomson in 1974/5, Marshall, Holding and Garner in any series since 1980. Such bowlers have seldom been dominated by batsmen for long, and they command special respect.

Bowlers confronted with the prospect of bowling to Viv Richards are often apprehensive or uneasy about the duel, but such feelings are nothing compared to the apprehension felt by batsmen about to face Malcolm Marshall. A truly fast bowler must enjoy limbering up each day and being greeted by sycophantic 'good mornings' from the opposition's more timorous batsmen. When a team arrives at a ground for the first day's play, the players always check up on the presence and/or fitness of the opposition's

Left *The most feared sight in modern cricket – Malcolm Marshall in full flight. Two points are worth noting: the ball is held in his fingers rather than the palm of his hand, and his head is ideally positioned to give him a clear view.*

Above *Australian pace bowler Terry Alderman looks as though he's about to fall over, but he won't. A serious shoulder injury in 1982 reduced his pace yet he continues to take wickets, proving that speed is not everything.*

'quickie'. Being a fast bowler has its compensations, then, but whether your name is Fred Root, Bob Willis or Dennis Lillee, it is hard work.

Joel Garner fancied himself as a batsman when a boy in the backyard (remarkably, he still does). Seymour Nurse, rather than Wes Hall, was his special hero, but as he became too tall to be a proper batsman his coach told him to put the bat down and concentrate on bowling. However, he did not begin as an express bowler but, to use his terms, as a 'medium pacer'; whether his opponents agreed with this assessment, I'm not sure. West Indian definitions of pace often bear little relation to those of the rest of the world. 'A bit sharp' according to a West Indian often means 'lightning fast' to the rest of us. Joel grew stronger and was finally tossed the new ball, the signal for any self respecting West Indian to bowl quickly. Especially in these days of the four-pronged pace attack, it is a matter of some pride to be entrusted with the new ball for the West Indies, so Joel started galloping up to the wicket like a rampaging giraffe.

When Graham Dilley attended winter nets with the Kent schools' team, it was as an unreliable medium pacer and batsman. Neil Taylor, now a middle-order batsman and occasional off spinner, used to open the bowling while Dilley was third change. Graham used to charge in as quickly as he could until, he said, 'my back went'. Two weeks later he returned to the nets, ran in very gingerly and suddenly coach Colin Page became very excited. By just

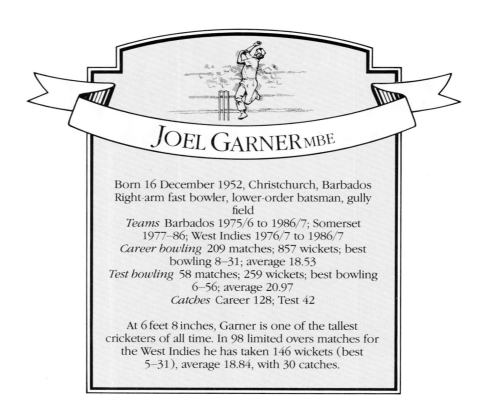

JOEL GARNER MBE

Born 16 December 1952, Christchurch, Barbados
Right-arm fast bowler, lower-order batsman, gully
field
Teams Barbados 1975/6 to 1986/7; Somerset
1977–86; West Indies 1976/7 to 1986/7
Career bowling 209 matches; 857 wickets; best
bowling 8–31; average 18.53
Test bowling 58 matches; 259 wickets; best bowling
6–56; average 20.97
Catches Career 128; Test 42

At 6 feet 8 inches, Garner is one of the tallest
cricketers of all time. In 98 limited overs matches for
the West Indies he has taken 146 wickets (best
5–31), average 18.84, with 30 catches.

relaxing and moving into the wicket more slowly, Dilley found greater pace. His batting has regressed ever since.

The same cannot be said of the world's leading Test wicket-taker, Ian Botham. While on the Lords' groundstaff he felt that his bowling was treated as a joke and he became very frustrated as a result, though I doubt whether he spent much time sulking in the corner of the dressing room. In 1974, Ian's first full season for Somerset, wicket-keeper Derek Taylor usually stood up to the wicket and Ian was regarded as a medium pace swing bowler. It wasn't until his first overseas tour to Pakistan that, finding the ball didn't swing much there, he tried to bowl quicker. Not everyone can make the transition from medium to fast, but Ian's natural strength and orthodox action allowed him to become extremely hostile for five years.

The two men who follow Botham in the Test wickets list took a different route to becoming pace bowlers. Both Dennis Lillee and Bob Willis began their first class careers as out and out fast bowlers. Lillee says,

'In those early days I sensed that pace and nothing else was to be my vehicle into first class cricket. But the age of 20 I was still little more than a tearaway kid who ran in perhaps too far and pounded the ball down just as fast as I could. I remember my length and direction came nowhere, but I also remember that not many of my team-mates were particularly worried about that because few batsmen were able to get into the loose stuff – I now appreciate that anyone who bowls at genuine pace can get away with just about anything most of the time.'

Bob Willis' career should be a great encouragement to potential fast bowlers, who have the coaches in despair. He describes himself,

'I'd be all jangling arms and legs; I'd be open-chested at the crucial moment of delivery; my follow through was a coach's nightmare yet the ball left my hand quickly.'

Both Lillee and Willis, one a paragon of orthodoxy, the other quite the reverse, gradually learnt to harness their ability to 'make the ball leave the hand quickly' to more subtle skills to become the backbone of their country's bowling attack for a decade.

The point I'm making is that there's no one well-trodden route to becoming a fast bowler. Some are fast at 19, others not until they are 24. Some have a superb action (and that undoubtedly helps) but others like Procter, Croft, Max Walker and Willis don't. In fact, an ungainly action has one distinct advantage; it's often very tricky to spot the ball amid a chaotic whirl of arms and feet. Michael Holding is a masterful bowler with an excellent action and he is very quick, but at least the batsman has a clear view of where the ball is coming from; not so when facing Mike Procter or Colin Croft for the first time – or the second, third or fourth, for that matter.

Joel Garner, a gentle giant of 6 feet 8 inches, makes the most of his height. In County cricket players often complained that the sight screens were too small when he was bowling. Batsmen can be unnerved by excessive pace and excessive bounce. When Garner combined the two, he could be lethal. The umpire, Don Oslear, is a strapping six-footer.

RUN UP AND ACTION

Not surprisingly, fast bowlers have different views on the ideal length of the run up. Joel Garner, whose run happens to be little more than 15 yards, reckons that '12–15 yards should be adequate, otherwise you'll be tired by the time you reach the wicket'. Bob Willis, whose run was a little longer, says, 'Don't worry about taking too long a run, provided it feels right.' Graham Dilley shortened his run from 40 yards to 25, without any great reduction of pace, because 'with the amount of cricket we play, I didn't think I'd last beyond my thirtieth birthday'. Once Gladstone Small decided to use little more than his Sunday League run he made the England side.

All, however, agree that the bowler should reach maximum speed during the last four or five strides of the run up. Garner says,

'Lots of bowlers have good run ups until they are five strides from the crease and then they lose it. They may as well run from four steps. In fact, the really good fast bowler can bowl quickly off five paces as they can get into their rhythm so quickly'.

I can vouch for this: when Malcolm Marshall opts for an 8-yard run, it's a mistake to sigh with relief.

At the end of the run up all that energy should be transferred into sending the ball to the other end swiftly and accurately. Ideally, this is what happens: the bowler,

Left Jeff Thomson bowling to David Gower in Brisbane; 1982. Thomson's dramatic catapult action stunned the cricket world, and the English batsmen in 1974/5. He was still a handful several years later in 1982. Batsmen found him extremely difficult to 'pick-up' since the ball was hidden behind his body up to the moment of delivery. This disguise together with his great pace made him a formidable opponent to face at the crease.

Above A purposeful Ian Botham bowling a bouncer against Pakistan at Headingley in 1982. When in his prime Botham never contemplated bowling a defensive ball. On the contrary, he was prepared to try any variation to claim a wicket. Such unpredictability and obvious aggressive intent often unsettled batsmen and, as a result, Botham has taken more wickets from 'mediocre' balls than any of his contemporaries.

holding the ball in his fingers rather than the palm of the hand, plants his back foot parallel to the crease while the front arm is thrust towards the sky; the hips rotate through 90°; the head is still, the front leg braced and the bowling arm high, before swinging down across the body and almost reaching the ground in the follow through. I'm not sure that anyone actually fulfils all these criteria completely, but that's the theory. Lillee, otherwise a magnificent model, didn't always brace his left leg; Willis was open-chested and Procter seemed to conjure up an action from nowhere while sprinting at full pace – so don't get depressed if the video shows you that you fail to match up to this checklist. Remember that a bowling action is a means to an end, and not an end in itself.

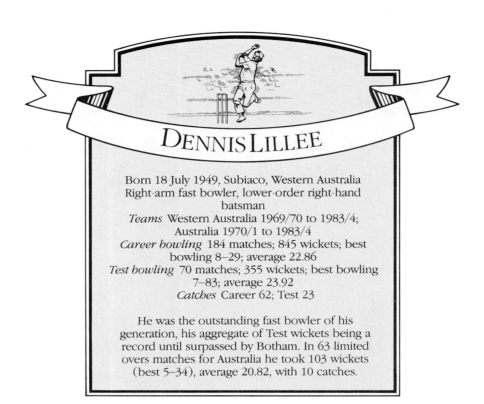

DENNIS LILLEE

Born 18 July 1949, Subiaco, Western Australia
Right-arm fast bowler, lower-order right-hand
batsman
Teams Western Australia 1969/70 to 1983/4;
Australia 1970/1 to 1983/4
Career bowling 184 matches; 845 wickets; best
bowling 8–29; average 22.86
Test bowling 70 matches; 355 wickets; best bowling
7–83; average 23.92
Catches Career 62; Test 23

He was the outstanding fast bowler of his
generation, his aggregate of Test wickets being a
record until surpassed by Botham. In 63 limited
overs matches for Australia he took 103 wickets
(best 5–34), average 20.82, with 10 catches.

Throughout their run up and action, all bowlers are striving for that elusive quality, rhythm. When fast bowlers have rhythm they find that the whole exercise becomes a little easier. When Botham's got rhythm, he says, 'Bowling is never laboured and I can bowl longer and longer because I'm taking less out of myself – I'm not charging in and putting everything into my delivery stride.' Dilley confirms this, adding, 'Since I don't feel I'm expending much energy, I often assume that I'm not bowling very quickly, but the keeper then tells me that I am.'

PREPARATION

I'm afraid that it is an inescapable fact that the fast bowler has to be the fittest member of the side; his is the most physically demanding role in the team and he is therefore the most vulnerable to injury. In 1974 Bob Willis overheard Ian Chappell say that if a batsman stayed in until after lunch against him, Willis was there for the taking. That hurt Willis who, to his credit, began an extensive running programme later in his career, which enabled him to bowl fast at 5.30 pm as well as 11.30 am. This programme also helped him continue his career long enough for him to take 325 Test wickets.

It is no coincidence that Dennis Lillee also committed himself to a rigorous training programme after breaking down in the West Indies in 1973. Lillee used a combination of running for stamina, flexibility exercises plus some simple strength exercises, like sit-ups, press-ups and squats; he also went into the weights room – but note that

it is vital for anyone intending to use weights to seek expert advice first. Finally he reckoned that regular swimming (and he wasn't very good at it) improved his fitness immeasurably. Fitness training has to be hard work to be of value, but for Lillee and Willis it was clearly worthwhile.

It is obviously important to ensure that you are loose on match days and that any niggling muscles are strapped up. Dilley, after group stretching, always bowls several deliveries in the nets to loosen up the relevant muscles further. In India in 1984, the English players found that Norman Cowans stiffened up during the 20 minutes before play began, so he was sent out just before the umpires to bowl on the outfield; his first over improved considerably as a result. When I asked Botham about preparation he pondered whether I was asking the right person, but even he will surreptitiously take the precaution of some stretching exercises before bowling.

Before going out on to the field make a habit of checking your boots – that they are properly studded and, if you drag like Dilley, that the toe caps are in good condition. A fast bowler should take particular care of his feet. In England especially, ensure that you have a vest and some sweaters in your case to keep you warm during and after a spell of bowling. I remember facing my first over in first class cricket from John Snow at The Parks in 1975. Thanks to a mixture of inside edge and front pad, I just survived. Snow was wearing five sweaters at the time.

Dennis Lillee displays the ideal follow through for an away swing bowler. He's close to the stumps; the right arm sweeps across the body and there's a devilish glint in his eye.

OPENING THE BOWLING

The first ball of a Test series produces a special tension; the spectators are on edge and their sympathies extend to the opening batsmen. They are the ones who have to go over the top first in the knowledge that an early mistake may have an utterly demoralizing effect that could last for the whole series. We tend to forget about the opening bowler; he's nervous as well. Inevitably the field is attacking – three slips, a gully and a forward short leg; the expectations of the fielders and the crowd are high; for the opening bowler there is little margin for error. Graham Dilley spearheaded England's attack in Australia in 1986/7 and he explains his approach.

'Apparently Frank Tyson aimed to bowl the fastest and best ball in his armoury first, but I slightly disagree with that. I'm feeling my way; despite all the loosening up, it's different in the middle. If you surrender the initiative in the first over by being wayward you may never get it back.'

Such a conservative approach is, of course, foreign to Ian Botham. He is aggressive from the start and wants to dominate the batsman at all costs. Like Lillee on the cricket pitch and Mohammad Ali in the ring, he has been able to gain a psychological ascendancy over his foe. He recalls one recent example where a mixture of the occasion and his presence made a wicket inevitable. 'At The Oval in 1986 the first ball on my comeback (after a two month ban) was always going to dismiss Bruce Edgar provided he had to play it. I think that even Edgar sensed this. I had the same feeling late in my spell against Australia at Edgbaston in 1981.' (Botham ended the innings with a 5–1 spell.) Unfortunately this deep inner confidence is not something that can be learnt and practised as can bowling or batting actions.

Where should the pace bowler aim to pitch his stock ball? 'In the corridor of uncertainty, of course,' replies Dilley. Dilley discovered this phrase, if not this strategy, from his former Kent colleague Terry Alderman: 'Where do you bowl, Terry?' – 'In the corridor, mate.' I believe that Alderman was introduced to this description by his former Western Australian captain John Inverarity.

Where is this corridor of uncertainty? It is a thin channel on, and just outside of, the off stump. When the ball lands in it the batsman should be unsure whether to play back or

Michael Holding is the most graceful and the most dignified of modern fast bowlers. Like Dennis Lillee later in his career, Holding sometimes cuts down his run to 10 paces, yet he is still able to torment batsmen.

forward – hence the uncertainty. It is a nice phrase, meaning bowling a line and length. Graeme Wood, when leading out Western Australia, expects his bowlers 'to hit the top of off stump'. A captain with a tautological turn of phrase might urge his attack to bowl 'in the corridor on a line and length and to hit the top of off stump' – all of which amounts to the same thing. Perhaps a more relevant point is that if a bowler can do this regularly he is accurate and if he is accurate he will take wickets.

However, true pace bowlers are not just simple bowling machines; they can sense the strengths and weaknesses of batsmen and make adjustments to their method of attack. Garner says that the West Indian bowlers are always probing and exposing weaknesses. At team meetings they discuss the opposition and how to bowl at them. 'If a man can't play the short ball, we'll bowl short all day at him; if he can't drive, we'll bowl fuller.'

Botham sometimes adopts the opposite strategy. 'When a player first comes in, I often like to bowl to his strength to encourage him to start playing his shots prematurely. To a good cover driver I might bowl full length outswingers and remove my mid-off. Hopefully he can't resist run-scoring opportunities before he is settled at the crease.'

Such a ploy can result in a flurry of boundaries, but Botham worries less about that than most; certainly it would not have appealed to Mike Hendrick, who was the epitome of accuracy. Hendrick was never such a prolific wicket taker for England yet he never bowled badly, whereas Botham, the gambler, has succeeded and failed spectacularly with the ball; take your choice.

Not even Botham, though, would pursue this policy blindly. For instance, when he bowled to Graeme Wood of Australia at the beginning of an innings he consciously tried to bowl maidens. He knew that Wood was a nervous starter who hated being on 0 and he reckoned that the longer he remained on 0 the greater the chance of dismissing him, even if it was from a run out after a desperate attempt at a short single.

Helpful wickets can sometimes undermine naïve fast bowlers. In the 1970s the Western Australia Cricket Association's pitch in Perth was reckoned to be the fastest in the world. Bowlers from the Eastern States of Australia would see the ball bouncing prodigiously, become extremely excited and start banging the ball in short. The sight of the wicketkeeper on tiptoe may have boosted their egos for a while but it produced few wickets. Meanwhile Lillee, Alderman and Malone bowled 'into the corridor' and kept bowling sides out. Joel Garner actually bowls slower sometimes if the wicket is helpful. 'I won't bowl as quickly as when the wicket is flat,' he says, 'but I'll concentrate in obtaining movement, bowling accurately and to a slightly fuller length. If that fails, then I'll try to blast them out.'

On flat, featherbed wickets, sheer pace may be the best solution. At The Oval Test in 1976 Michael Holding took 14–149 in one of the most awesome exhibitions of fast bowling of modern times. Neither the wicket nor the atmosphere offered him any assistance, so he decided to bowl fast and straight and the Englishmen could not pick up the ball in time. Remarkably, Imran Khan once ex-pressed a preference for the Eastbourne wicket, which is slow and low as compared to the bounce and movement of Hove. If he beat the bat at Hove the ball invariably bounced over the stumps, at Eastbourne it hit them. (I'm not sure that many pace bowlers would agree with his assessment, however.)

The spinners will set great store on their ability to outwit their opponents. Fast bowlers are allowed to think as well and they are generally even more eager to let you know when they've out-thought a batsman instead of just blasting him out. The sensible response is to nod politely.

Yorker

The fast bowler has two deliveries in his armoury which land nowhere near 'the corridor' – the yorker and the bouncer. The yorker is a fast, straight ball that pitches on the popping crease where the batsman is standing before smashing into the stumps. Not every fast bowler can master it. Lillee rarely bowled a good yorker but Jeff Thomson did. It is particularly effective against a batsman who has just arrived at the crease.

The modern master of the yorker is Joel Garner. In County cricket I've witnessed Garner size up a new batsman. He bowls three balls just short of a length, so that the batsman is set in a rhythm of standing high on his back foot, then suddenly the yorker zooms in. The batsman is stranded on his back foot and the stumps (or maybe his toes) are shattered. Bowlers should swiftly learn which batsmen are susceptible to the yorker and which are capable of making it into a full toss. In 1974/5 the Australians soon spotted that Tony Greig, with his upright stance and long frame, had great difficulty dealing with Thomson's 'sandshoe crusher'. John Edrich, about a yard nearer the ground, handled it rather better.

Bouncer

The bouncer has always provoked controversy, whether in the era of Larwood or Lillee. In his autobiography *Back to The Mark*, Lillee wrote that he aimed to hit batsmen when he sent down short pitched deliveries and as a result the cricket world debated the topic at length. In fact, Dilley and Botham say the same, but omit the words 'to hit'. They aim at exactly the same spot as Lillee does, so it seems to me that the difference in approach is minimal. Dilley has said: 'To bowl a good bouncer you have to aim it at the head and upper body. Now the worst thing in the world is seeing

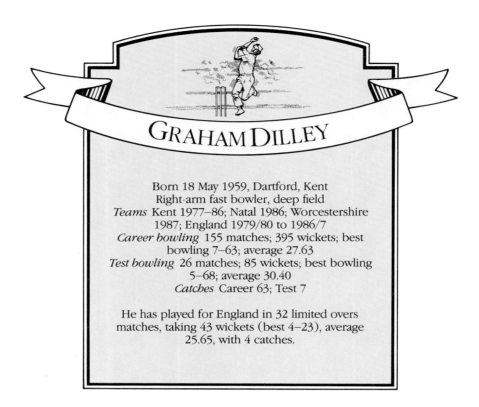

GRAHAM DILLEY

Born 18 May 1959, Dartford, Kent
Right-arm fast bowler, deep field
Teams Kent 1977–86; Natal 1986; Worcestershire
1987; England 1979/80 to 1986/7
Career bowling 155 matches; 395 wickets; best
bowling 7–63; average 27.63
Test bowling 26 matches; 85 wickets; best bowling
5–68; average 30.40
Catches Career 63; Test 7

He has played for England in 32 limited overs
matches, taking 43 wickets (best 4–23), average
25.65, with 4 catches.

someone lying on the ground with blood pouring out, but you have to aim it somewhere and that is the most effective spot. The batsman might fend it off to the slips or short-leg or he might mishook; at least he might become a little more apprehensive about facing the next ball.'

Dilley, like Garner, prefers to use the bouncer sparingly as a shock weapon. If, however, they spot a batsman starting to lunge forward to negate any movement off the wicket they won't hesitate to use it straight away. Sometimes Dilley bowls a bouncer purely for his own benefit. If I'm bowling too full, I often bowl a bouncer to help me rediscover my length and to remind myself that I'm not supposed to be bowling half volleys all the time.'

Botham has probably bowled more bouncers in his career than any other bowler of similar pace and his views are predictably forthright: 'Some people say that if a batsman doesn't hook, it's a waste of time bouncing them. I think that's rubbish. You have to make every batsman wonder "what's he going to bowl to me now?" Also, even the best hookers can get out to the bouncer. I've got Viv Richards out with a bouncer as well as being smashed by him. Against good hookers, I try to get the bouncer a little higher.' I'm not sure whether Botham should be held up as a model for ordinary mortals in this regard, but there's no doubt that his bouncer has had a mesmeric effect on batsmen – think of Australia's Andrew Hilditch in 1985.

The likes of Lillee, Roberts and Marshall all had two bouncers, which is an extremely devious ploy. The first, of normal pace, the batsman might hook to the boundary, feel an upsurge in confidence and conclude that 'this chap is not as quick as they all make out'. The second bouncer is

appreciably quicker, and if he tries to hook this one he might be in for a nasty shock.

Finally, a typically pragmatic note from Joel Garner. 'Bowling bouncers takes extra energy. If you bowl a lot you are going to lose out on those final overs at the end of the day. I find it more satisfying to bowl batsmen out rather than scare them.'

Swing/seam

Sheer pace is not always enough. A few years ago, Alan Knott told Graham Dilley that the only way you can consistently get good players out is to move the ball away. Dilley listened and has worked hard to cultivate a genuine outswinger. In Australia in 1986/7 he was dismissing good players regularly. For Botham the away swinger came naturally. The advantages of swinging the ball are obvious; if a bowler can swing the ball in the air he is no longer so dependent on the nature of the playing surface .

For an away swinger, the ball should be held in the fingers with the seam pointing towards first slip and the shiny side on the right (for a right handed bowler). The ball should be delivered from close to the stumps, in a side-on position with the bowling arm coming across the body – in other words, the perfect bowling action described earlier. Dilley often ensures that he is staying side on by checking the position of his feet in the delivery stride. He says, 'If they are in a straight line, ie not open, then I should get my upper body round and I should have a chance of swinging it.'

Graham Dilley relies more on swing than speed.

GRIPS FOR SWING

Why cricket balls swing has always mystified me, but they do.
Here are the conventional grips.

Right For away/out swing the ball is held so that the seam is vertical and pointing towards first slip. The first and second fingers are placed either side of the seam with the edge of the thumb on the seam.

Right For inswing the vertical seam points towards fine leg. The first and second fingers are close together either side of the vertical seam. The ball of the thumb is flat against the underside of the seam.

Open-chested bowlers tend to bowl inswingers. These are usually delivered from wide of the crease, with the bowling arm ending up between the bowler's legs or on the right hand side of his body. The ball is held with the shiny side on the left and the seam heading for fine leg. Later in his career, Botham developed the inswinger as his action became a little more open-chested and he has tried hard to disguise it. He makes one crucial observation for swing bowlers: 'If the ball is swinging it is vital to bowl a fuller length, to give the ball a chance.' Bowlers with fluid wrist actions like Bob Massie in his prime and Richard Hadlee seem able to swing the ball later in its trajectory.

Effective seam bowlers have the happy knack of ensuring that the ball lands on its seam and deviates as a result. They try to ensure that the seam stays perpendicular on its journey down the wicket and on a receptive surface something should happen, although not even the best of seamers are certain of exactly what it will be. Mike Hendrick, a quality international bowler, could never predict which way the ball would move – and nor, of course, could the batsman.

The more ambitious among you may like to attempt some cutters, at least in the nets. Alec Bedser was a master of the leg cutter and, later in his career, so was Dennis Lillee, using them to great effect from a shortened run. Gripping the ball along the seam with fingers slightly apart, you bring your hand and fingers through on the left-hand side of the ball to impart spin from leg to off. For the off cutter, the hand and fingers come down on the right hand side of the ball. In *The Art of Fast Bowling*, Lillee offers one vital cautionary note: 'Bowling cutters requires an entirely different hand movement to that used for swingers and a great killer of swing is when the bowler loses the ability to let the ball go with his hand and fingers behind the ball right through the delivery.' So beware.

If all of the above fails, change of pace and use of the crease can deceive the batsman. I've already mentioned how Holding employed change of pace at The Oval in 1976 – instead of bowling quick, he bowled lightning fast, but

that option will be denied to most of you. However, a slower ball is a useful ploy provided it is well disguised and accurate. A decrease in pace should occur if the ball is held further down in the palm of the hand, rather than in the fingers. If nothing else, it keeps the batsmen guessing. Finally, it's not beyond a fast bowler's dignity to frustrate batsmen out. I say this because Garner has told me how he and Marshall on good wickets have cut down their pace and simply worn the batsmen down by giving them nothing to hit – 'rather than killing yourself to get them, they've got to get you'. Once the breakthrough has been achieved they step up a gear and start attacking again.

PROBLEMS

John Lever of Essex bowls a no ball once a decade, Botham once a season, and Garner and Willis probably once every four overs. Gladstone Small once bowled an 18 ball over. No balls drive captains who are batsmen round the bend – 'just put your mark back a few feet' is their standard suggestion, but obviously it's not as simple as that.

Bob Willis, even when he had 300 Test wickets to his name, used to march out to the wicket before the match with Norman Gifford and a tape measure. They would measure his run up to the nearest centimetre, yet he still bowled no balls. In the famous 1981 Headingley Test, Brearley instructed Willis (8–43) to forget about no balls. All-out attack was required; there was no point in sacrificing pace for precision. It would be like a tennis player worrying about foot faults when he's 0–40 down at the end of the fifth set. However, in normal situations, and especially in limited overs cricket, no balls are a terrible waste of resources. Willis never completely resolved the problem, though it's interesting to note that he found long jump practice a useful exercise, helping him to time the sprint and stopping him overstraining in the last few strides.

By his own admission, Garner also bowls too many no balls: 'They usually come when I'm searching for extra

MEDIUM AWAY SWINGER TO RIGHT-HAND BATSMAN

An away/out swing bowler should be played into the off side as he aims to pitch the ball around off stump, hoping to induce an edge to the wicketkeeper or slips, so there are just three fielders on the leg side. If the bowler is in control, 4 might strengthen the slip cordon thereby increasing the chances of a catch.

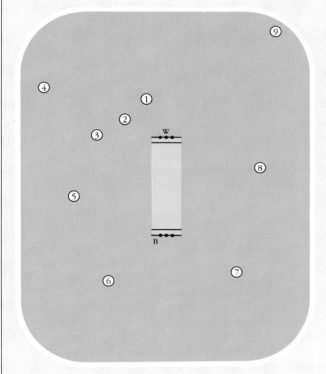

Key: 1, first slip; 2, second slip; 3, gully; 4, third man; 5, cover point; 6, mid-off; 7, mid-on; 8, square leg; 9, long leg.

INSWING BOWLER TO RIGHT-HAND BATSMAN

For an inswing bowler the majority of fielders will be on the leg side. If the ball is swinging into him the batsman is likely to play the ball to leg.

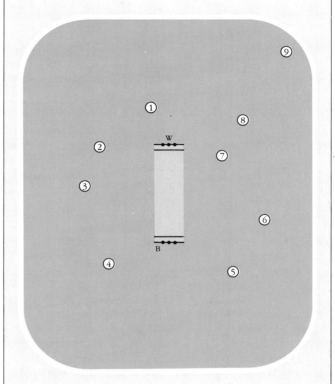

Key: 1, third man; 2, cover point; 3, deep cover; 4, extra cover; 5, mid-off: 6, mid-on; 7, mid-wicket; 8, deep backward square-leg; 9, long leg.

pace: I may be frustrated by not taking wickets and I lose my rhythm and concentration. Even if I add a yard to my run, I still stretch out and overstep, so usually I try reducing my run up by half a yard; I run up to the wicket slower and hopefully I stop stretching for the crease.' It remains a mystery to pure batsmen why bowlers have to be as close to the other end as possible; they don't understand why the bowlers can't leave a six-inch safety gap.

On some days that 'corridor' will prove elusive and Dilley suggests, 'You should realize this quickly and adjust until your confidence returns. There's no point having three slips and two gullies if you don't know where the ball is going to land.' A few times in his career Dilley has suffered more long-term setbacks through loss of fitness and form: 'Somehow you have to retain a belief in your own ability and recognize that you've done it in the past. Also, I've found that a complete break of, say, a fortnight has helped me to relax more.'

The West Indians are reckoned to be masters at the art

of relaxation. If so, Garner is a shining example. His record for Somerset and the West Indies on the 'big' occasion is remarkable.

'I have developed a pattern before important matches, though I wouldn't advocate it for younger fellas. Once I decided to go to sleep early before a big match. I tossed and turned all night and arrived at the ground exhausted, having played the whole game through in my mind. So ever since then I've kept to a routine. I may not get home until 1 or 2 am, having had a few drinks with friends – maybe four or five, rather than 10 – and then I get six good hours sleep rather than nine restless ones. In the morning, once I put my tracksuit on, I start thinking about the game and I expect to bowl well and be successful. If I'm bowling to a good player, like Graham Gooch, I still feel confident. It needs just one ball to get him out, but it takes him a lot of balls to get 100.'

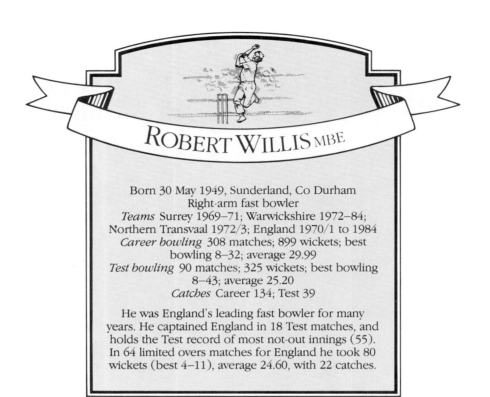

ROBERT WILLIS MBE

Born 30 May 1949, Sunderland, Co Durham
Right-arm fast bowler
Teams Surrey 1969–71; Warwickshire 1972–84;
Northern Transvaal 1972/3; England 1970/1 to 1984
Career bowling 308 matches; 899 wickets; best
bowling 8–32; average 29.99
Test bowling 90 matches; 325 wickets; best bowling
8–43; average 25.20
Catches Career 134; Test 39

He was England's leading fast bowler for many
years. He captained England in 18 Test matches, and
holds the Test record of most not-out innings (55).
In 64 limited overs matches for England he took 80
wickets (best 4–11), average 24.60, with 22 catches.

I'm not suggesting that all potential fast bowlers should emulate Garner's lifestyle. The point is that they should stick to their normal routine before an important match, rather than slavishly follow what is expected of them. This might entail a piping hot cup of Horlicks at 9.30 pm followed by a chapter of Jane Austen before retiring early, though from my experience of fast bowlers this is a trifle unlikely.

LIMITED OVERS

Joel Garner has become one of the most successful limited overs bowlers ever, which is hardly surprising: he is extremely accurate, he obtains unusual bounce and he can be 'fast'. Usually he takes the new ball in limited overs games and his first four or five overs will not differ much from a County or Test match. Obviously there will be fewer attacking fieldsmen, but he is still looking for edges and aiming to dismiss batsmen. With the introduction of the circle in limited overs matches (see the diagram on p.116), one of the most inspired of recent changes in the laws, it is increasingly important to take wickets early in an innings.

However, at the end of an innings he might make considerable adjustments. If the fielding side is still on top he'll continue to hunt for wickets; but if the batsmen are in a position of strength and able to swing indiscriminately, he tries to bowl leg stump yorkers, interspersed with the odd short ball to stop the batsman premeditating. His aim is to prevent the batsman from swinging his bat freely, and

as he approaches the wicket he keeps an eye on him to check whether he is moving.

He will occasionally practise adjusting his length in the nets. When he began he used to bowl at a piece of paper on a good length, but now, in this multi-coloured one-day world, he practises three lengths; a yorker, a normal length, and short of a length. He will get someone to call out to him which length to hit as he reaches the end of his run up, thereby simulating adjustment to a batsman's late movement.

Botham adopts a similar plan at the end of an innings, aiming to bowl well up on middle and leg stump, but Dilley has discovered that he's more expensive trying to bowl 'blockhole' balls and so he retains his normal line and length. Since this is a little shorter than most and as he has a little extra pace he finds that these deliveries are not usually in the 'slogging arc'. Whatever length the bowlers choose, they all agree that it is vital to hit the stumps if the batsman misses.

Once you have mastered all of the above, all you need to become a great fast bowler, according to a few coaching manuals I have looked at, are limitless reserves of stamina, resilience, endurance, aggression, optimism, courage and determination. It's no wonder there aren't too many of them around.

Pace bowlers once had a code whereby they wouldn't 'bounce' one another. As this photograph demonstrates, this code no longer applies. Geoff Lawson has managed to evade a bouncer from Bob Willis, but he looks distinctly uncomfortable and he's taken his eye off the ball.

THE SPINNER

The total domination of world cricket by the West Indies, plus the advent of so much limited overs cricket, has threatened the status of the spinner in recent years. When Malcolm Marshall or Joel Garner are replaced by Roger Harper in the West Indian attack it is hardly surprising that most batsmen breathe a quiet sigh of relief. Fortunately for cricket and cricketers, no other side in the world can call upon such an effective battery of fast bowlers, and for every other team the role of the spinner remains vital.

Middlesex and Essex, the two most successful English County sides of the last decade, have prospered because they have a balanced attack, capable of exploiting any conditions. Emburey and Edmonds and a combination of Acfield, East and Childs have contributed as much to their team's success as Daniel and Cowans, Lever and Foster. The presence of Edmonds and Emburey makes the English bowling attack more versatile and effective than its Australian counterpart. In Pakistan, Abdul Qadir has caused havoc among the West Indian batsmen, and Bob Holland is still being selected for New South Wales and touted for Australia at the age of 40.

Spinners can't hurt a batsman, but they can certainly intimidate him. Facing Abdul Qadir in Karachi surrounded by a cluster of fieldsmen hovering like vultures is no picnic, especially if you don't know which way the ball will bounce. I know this from bitter personal experience. For 15 minutes I was utterly bamboozled by Qadir's variations, then mercifully his googly bowled me and, downcast, I headed for the pavilion. My mood was not improved when some time later I read in a newspaper, 'I don't know what Marks read at Oxford, but it certainly wasn't wrist spin'.

Being humiliated can sometimes be as painful as being hit. Brian Rose of Somerset recalls a feeling of dread when facing Fred Titmus for the first time. For a start, he could see no way in which he could score a run because of the great man's control; in addition, Peter Parfitt and John Murray behind the stumps were chattering away in a manner not designed to help the 18-year-old's confidence.

Australian glee as off spinner Bruce Yardley dismisses Derek Randall in Perth in 1982. Even the first seagull seems to be appealing. Yardley was nicknamed 'Roo' because of the huge leaps of delight that followed every wicket he took. He was an unusual off spinner since he spun the ball with his second finger rather than his index finger.

Below *Abdul Qadir, currently the world's best leg spinner, who is a delight to watch but very embarrassing to play against.*

Above *In the Sixties and Seventies Kent used to take Derek Underwood around with them like an umbrella – just in case of rain. His pinpoint accuracy and speed through the air made him lethal on wet wickets. In 1987 uncovered wickets returned to English County cricket and 'Deadly Derek' was still playing and still as lethal.*

The likes of Tony Lock, Norman Gifford and Phil Edmonds can create a mood of aggression and hostility even if they are bowling at less than 50 mph, while the knowing glance of a Laker or an Emburey suggests that you will be trapped in their web. Underwood on a turning wicket is so relentless that he induces the sort of claustrophobia we associate with prisoners of war; desperate attempts at escape usually result in failure.

Spinners bring charm and subtlety to the game, creating a duel that is more mental than physical, which is perhaps why they take longer to mature as bowlers. In English County cricket in 1986 40 per cent of the regular spinners were aged 35 or over and concern about the whereabouts of young spinners was well founded. Legislators around the world have attempted to aid their survival by introducing minimum over rates, but it is the groundsmen who hold the key; a good wicket should start to favour the spinners on the last two days of a match.

THE TECHNIQUE

Few of the experts I talked to started life as spin bowlers. At the age of 11 Pat Pocock wanted to 'run in and bowl as fast

GRIPS FOR SPIN

It is much easier to be an adequate off spinner than leg spinner, less satisfying though.

Right For off spin the seam is at right angles to the widely spaced first and second fingers. The top joints of the fingers are on the seam.

Right For leg spin/break the seam is at right angles to the comfortably spaced first and second fingers. The top joint of the third finger lies along the seam.

as I could'. Phil Edmonds, as a youngster in Zambia, described himself as 'Left arm over and viciously quick' and added, with a twinkle in his eye, 'Having seen some of England's performances, I should have undoubtedly pursued that career.' John Emburey bowled medium pace outswingers as a 10-year-old. He spent a lot of time playing cricket across the street: 'We used to bowl at the kerb, which would be around a good length; if you hit it the batsman was stuffed.' Emburey believes that this training ground enabled him to achieve a mastery of line and length which, 20 years later, is the cornerstone of his bowling. Norman Gifford says he can't remember the details of his early efforts.

A 10-year-old rarely has sufficiently long fingers to impart spin to the ball, so at this age it is better to concentrate on developing a smooth, rhythmical action. There's no point in deciding too early what type of bowler you want to be; examine every option. Eddie Hemmings didn't switch to off spin until his late twenties; Bruce Yardley also began his first class career as a medium pacer. Indeed, the ideal action is the same as for an away swinger. Pat Pocock likens the whole procedure to a cartwheel: 'Your front leg, front arm, head, bowling arm and following leg should all go through the same line just like a cartwheel, giving you direction, pace off the wicket and consistency. You are creating a much longer aiming machine – after all, a rifle is more accurate than a small pistol.'

The ball should be held in the fingers rather than the palm of the hand and the spin imparted by the index finger. You can practise the action simply by flicking the ball into the air with the index finger. Gradually the process becomes automatic. If I had to bowl at the stumps to decide a rain-ruined one-day game (heaven forbid), I would do so bowling off spinners rather than 'seam-up', as that has become the natural way to deliver the ball for me.

An off spinner (or a left armer bowling over the wicket) should try to bowl from as close to the stumps as possible. John Emburey's front foot has always landed in front of the middle and leg stumps. In the late 1970s Pat Pocock concentrated on getting closer to the stumps and quickly realized the advantages. Any ball that pitches on the stumps should hit them, provided it doesn't turn (that happens quite frequently), and cognizant umpires should be on the lookout for LBW. Also, the swinger doesn't have to swing so much to be effective and the ball is less likely to be hit through the off side.

Ideally, then, a spinner bowling over the wicket has a perfect away swinger's action; he bowls from close to the stumps, pivoting as high as possible on his front foot and – very important – he should follow through. It is a grave mistake for slow bowlers to think that theirs is an occupation that requires little effort. Even though you are delivering the ball relatively slowly, it must have energy on it. Phil Edmonds in self-critical mood explains:

'One of my faults is that I'm a bit lazy and I don't have a tremendous follow through; sometimes I just flop it there and that allows the batsman to take the initiative. When I'm keyed up, however, I try to visualize my body going right through in my action and the ball going up in the air, dipping down, bouncing and hitting the splice of the bat.'

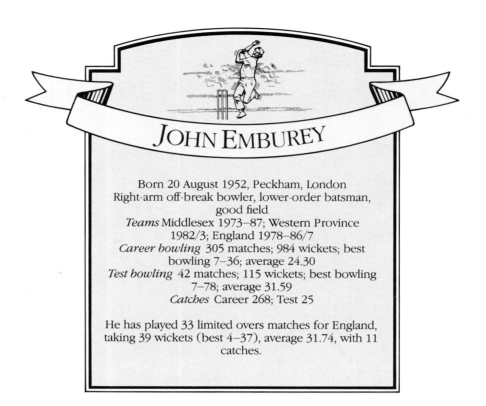

JOHN EMBUREY

Born 20 August 1952, Peckham, London
Right-arm off-break bowler, lower-order batsman,
good field
Teams Middlesex 1973–87; Western Province
1982/3; England 1978–86/7
Career bowling 305 matches; 984 wickets; best
bowling 7–36; average 24.30
Test bowling 42 matches; 115 wickets; best bowling
7–78; average 31.59
Catches Career 268; Test 25

He has played 33 limited overs matches for England,
taking 39 wickets (best 4–37), average 31.74, with 11
catches.

Obviously it is an advantage to have an orthodox, classical action, like Edmonds, but it is not essential. Pocock cites Norman Gifford as an example; 'He does very little right, but he's taken 1,900 wickets.' Gifford himself concedes that his delivery stride is too long so that he doesn't maximize his height, but he reckons that after the age of 14 it is very difficult to change a bowling action significantly and it's simply a question of making the most of what you have. For Gifford, rhythm is the key; in fact, all bowlers constantly refer to rhythm but find it hard to define. When you've got it, bowling becomes a simple operation; everything is effortless and the ball lands in the right place at the right pace. Gifford says that when he has rhythm he feels comfortable at the end of his mark, not just at the crease. The run up is not too fast, not too slow and the whole process feels like 'having a piece of carpet, holding one end and letting the other roll out; bowling becomes automatic and you don't have to think about which foot starts your run up, just set off'.

Yet the best of bowlers can lose their rhythm. Both Edmonds and Gifford have experienced 'the stutters'. In India in 1984, Edmonds lost his run up and wandered up to the wicket like an indecisive duck on a river bank contemplating the advantages of a swim. Fortunately, because he has an excellent action and a strong arm, his bowling was scarcely affected. Gifford has also been compelled to retreat to the nets and, experiencing considerable mental torture, has tried to identify which foot sets off first. Between them these two have bowled over 30,000 overs, so don't be too despondent if your run up occasionally goes awry.

PLANNING THE ATTACK

A spinner has to live by his wits and his mind should be alert and active well before the captain has summoned him to bowl. First, it is a good idea to assess the lengths of the boundaries at each end and the direction of the breeze. Pat Pocock even checks the quality of the background, as he reckons that bowling from a poor background increases the chances of deception. Most spinners prefer to bowl with long boundaries straight and on the leg side. Modern batmakers have not aided the spinner's cause and regrettably a mishit can easily carry for six at the old Pavilion End at Taunton, so I always try to bowl the other end. However, off spinners generally prefer to bowl with the wind blowing from the leg to the off side; this helps to drift the ball like a gentle away swinger before it spins back. Even if the ball doesn't turn, there's a chance of an edge to slip or perhaps an LBW decision from an ill-considered sweep shot.

These factors should help the spinner decide which end he should bowl. Of course the best laid plans can easily be scuppered by the captain, who also has to keep his temperamental fast bowler happy. But should he offer a choice of ends, a decisive 'Pavilion end, please' is far more convincing than 'I don't mind, I haven't really thought about it'.

John Emburey, England's leading off spinner, bowling at Old Trafford in 1985. Note how his left leg lands in front of leg stump. By being so close to the stumps a bowler's chances of an LBW decision are greatly enhanced.

The next consideration is the state of play and the nature of the opposition. Obviously, if the score is 150–0 you are less likely to have as many attacking fielders than if it is 60–3; however, I'll discuss the details of field placements later. Knowledge of your opponents is very helpful. Ray Illingworth was blessed with a 'photostat brain'; after observing one innings he could recall whether a batsman was a good cutter or driver and whether he swept. Norman Gifford suggests that those with poorer memories should keep a little black book in which to record a batsman's likes and dislikes.

Let me give a couple of examples. Whenever I bowl at Mike Gatting – not a pastime I particularly relish – I know that he likes to make room to cut through the off side early in his innings. Often he will feint to come down the wicket to induce me to pitch shorter; so I try to bowl very straight and reasonably full. Unfortunately, Gatting is sufficiently gifted to carry out those threats of leaping down to drive later in his innings. Similarly, when John Emburey bowls to David Gower he tries to tuck him up. One of Gower's favourite shots against the off spinner is the square cut/flash to anything wide of the stumps. Therefore Emburey tries to prevent him playing that shot; just occasionally he may bowl a wider, slower delivery in the knowledge that something is liable to happen – perhaps a snick, perhaps a four.

Finally, a spinner will try to assess the wicket, if only out of curiosity. A dry crumbly surface or a damp one is most likely to make the ball grip and turn, whereas a firm, well grassed surface is less helpful for spin. However, it is best not to be too dogmatic. Wickets all over the world have fooled cricket sages for years. One golden rule – never admit that the ball is turning unless you're taking wickets.

LINE AND LENGTH

The time has come for the spinner's first over. All those I spoke to have the same goal in mind – to find their line and length straightaway and to exert pressure on the batsman. Even Pat Pocock, who is renowned as a great experimenter who loves to flirt with every possible variation, claims that in his first two overs he is not too ambitious: 'I don't expect to get a wicket straightaway; I just want to establish a base.' I interviewed Pat during a lengthy cloudburst at Taunton when Somerset played Surrey. The following day I

faced his first over and was a little surprised to receive two arm balls, one from wide of the crease, plus a slower ball, all in the space of six balls. He sheepishly explained that it was the last over before lunch so that his theories had to go briefly out of the window. Derek Underwood once self-deprecatingly described himself as a 'low mentality bowler'; ie, he took very few risks and concentrated upon relentless accuracy. Pocock's mind is too inventive and restless for that and, understandably, this characteristic is often displayed in his bowling.

Norman Gifford works on the principle that when he takes the ball, both he and the batsman have a 50 per cent chance of success. Initially he tries to tilt the balance in his favour by preventing the batsman from scoring. He doesn't experiment or vary his deliveries at first; he wants to pressurize the batsman to make him wonder where he's going to score his runs, thereby forcing him to take risks and, hopefully, make an error. Emburey adopts the same philosophy: 'I begin bowling quicker and flatter; by the third or fourth over I may slow down a little until I find the right pace for the wicket. I don't look to take wickets initially, though I'll still have men around the bat in case the batsman makes a misjudgement.' Edmonds declares, 'Maybe I'm naïve, but I always expect my first over to be a maiden.' A sense of injustice pervades if it isn't.

It's clearly a good policy to aim for maiden overs early in your spell in order to make the batsman fidgety and impatient for runs. The vast majority of spinners' wickets come from batsmen's errors rather than unplayable balls, and a good batsman is unlikely to make any mistakes if he's assured of one long hop per over. If Richard Hadlee bowls the perfect leg cutter pitching on leg stump and hitting the off, he can expect a wicket maybe 80 per cent of the time; more often than not the perfect off spinner hits the batsman's pad harmlessly. So spinners have to rely more on the cumulative effect of several overs of sustained pressure to gain their wickets.

I've glibly referred to slow bowlers striving to gain control of their line and length early in their spell, but what is meant by 'line and length'? Pocock believes that it should be relatively easy for professional spinners to bowl a good line, and adds, 'You can stray in length and get away with it if your line is right.' What is the right line? An off spinner bowling on a good wicket to a right handed batsman should normally aim to pitch the ball on or just outside the off stump so that it will hit the wicket if the batsman misses.

Anything wider, especially on slow, low-bouncing wickets, is liable to be smashed through the off side unless the length is absolutely perfect. Anything wide of leg stump provides the batsman with a free hit. A left-arm spinner bowling to a right handed batsman will usually aim to hit off stump.

A good length cannot be pinpointed so easily since it depends whether you are bowling to Joel Garner or Allan Lamb. Basically the ball should induce the batsman to play forward (preferably after some hesitation) without him being able to hit it on the half volley.

Below *Derek Underwood about to deliver. The umpire is recognizable as Swaroop Kishan of India. Forward short leg remains anonymous; it's not Gatting.*

Right *John Emburey displays the perfect follow through for an off spin bowler with the left leg braced and the right arm swinging across his body; Adelaide, 1986.*

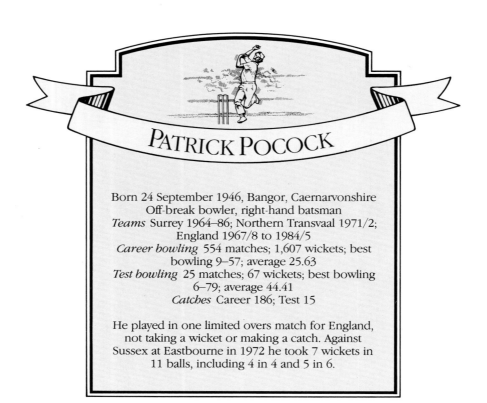

PATRICK POCOCK

Born 24 September 1946, Bangor, Caernarvonshire
Off-break bowler, right-hand batsman
Teams Surrey 1964–86; Northern Transvaal 1971/2;
England 1967/8 to 1984/5
Career bowling 554 matches; 1,607 wickets; best
bowling 9–57; average 25.63
Test bowling 25 matches; 67 wickets; best bowling
6–79; average 44.41
Catches Career 186; Test 15

He played in one limited overs match for England,
not taking a wicket or making a catch. Against
Sussex at Eastbourne in 1972 he took 7 wickets in
11 balls, including 4 in 4 and 5 in 6.

Once control has been established, there is then the option of introducing a few variations of flight and pace. These should be neither too frequent nor too pronounced. Remember also that since we are not machines, variations will occur unintentionally.

Pat Pocock, having observed faster bowlers bowling off spinners in the nets, remarks, 'Their slower ball is almost a lob; there is a difference between lobbing the ball and flighting it. It is even more important to put body into a slower ball so that it dips at the end of its flight.' Edmonds confirms this: 'A slower ball needs more effort or you'll end up bowling lollipops.' The arm action should remain the same, but the quicker ball should be released later with the wrist cocked back more; the slower ball should be released earlier and higher. Experiment in the nets. If the batsman is misjudging and mistiming the ball, you are winning.

Another weapon is the much publicized 'arm ball'. I suspect that these are bowled rather less frequently than some TV commentators would have us believe. They often attribute every ball that doesn't spin as an intentional 'arm ball'; in fact they are generally simply non-turning off breaks. The best exponent of the arm ball in English cricket is John Emburey. He simply bowls an away swinger, but he doesn't change his grip; he keeps his index finger behind the ball rather than flicking it to impart spin and his wrist remains unbroken. Ideally the ball sets off at leg stump, committing the batsman to sweep; it swings in the air and he is LBW or bowled. Emburey's perfect away swing action, plus those years of practice as a child, has meant that he has bamboozled many batsmen, particularly tailenders, with his arm ball. But don't worry if your action doesn't produce swing. Jack Birkenshaw, a highly successful off spinner for Leicestershire and England, never bowled an arm ball in his life.

A left handed bowler delivering to a right handed batsman often bowls his arm ball appreciably quicker, starting it outside the off stump. The batsman senses a chance to cut, moves into position, but is undone by the pace of the ball and the swing. He is bowled. That, at least, is the theory. Edmonds has a good arm ball, Underwood a better one. It is best not to use it too frequently; keep it as a surprise weapon and don't become obsessed by it. Pocock recalls helping in a coaching film and spending 25 per cent of the time on the swinger; in his view its importance was over-emphasized, since he believes that a young spinner should concentrate first on getting as much left to right spin as possible.

Variety can also be introduced by changing the point of delivery. An off spinner might bowl around the wicket, not because of prodigious turn, but simply to alter the angle of attack. A left-arm spinner might bowl over the wicket to pitch the ball in the bowler's footmarks. If a batsman appears set in a rhythm it is worth trying any legitimate ploy to upset it – provided it is not at the expense of your own accuracy.

Pat Pocock, in contrast to John Emburey, was a restless, eager off spinner, always prepared to experiment. Here he is seen bowling in Delhi (1984) where the ground was so hard that he opted not to wear studs. The photograph illustrates well the orthodox grip for an off spinner.

SETTING THE FIELD

The positioning of the fieldsmen is absolutely fundamental to a spinner's success and every spinner should have a clear picture of the field he would like when he starts his spell. This then becomes a matter of debate with the captain. Sometimes there will be disagreements; John Emburey has been known to point out to his captain in the friendliest of terms: 'Gatt, I just can't bowl to this field.' Edmonds has admitted to becoming 'very frustrated' if the captain insists he knows best. He gives one example: 'Mike Brearley never understood my concept of the in/out field, partly because of how he batted. I often liked to bowl with a long-off instead of a mid-off, especially when I had men around the bat. I don't think too many batters are adept at pushing the ball for one on the off side. A long-off prevented any straight boundaries and there was an outside chance of a catch if the batsman panicked. Also, the position encouraged the batsman to push at the ball to gain a single, thereby increasing the chances of a caught and bowled.' It is easy to understand the two lines of thought. I doubt whether Brearley was ever caught at long off in his life, but he was an excellent manipulator of the ball; he would much prefer to face Edmonds bowling with a long-off rather than a mid-off. Edmonds the batsman is a hitter or a blocker; he has been caught at long-off several times in his career, hence he regards long-off as an attacking position.

It is important for the captain and the spin bowler to understand each other's aims, and captains are usually prepared to accede to their spinner's demands. The keynote for both parties is to be flexible and sensitive to a particular batsman's strengths and weaknesses. Two batsmen rarely require identical fields.

At first class level it is extremely common to see a spinner operating with a silly point and a short-square leg no more than 5 feet from the bat. These fielding positions have emerged over the last 15 years as a result of a change in batting technique. Now, when defending, players often place their bats behind their front leg; if they are deceived the ball is most likely to pop up in front of the wicket.

In addition, these close fielders are reckoned to put pressure upon a timid batsman; the presence of a scowling, fearless fieldsman (say Brian Close) near enough to tickle your armpit is not designed to aid concentration. First class cricket apart, I strongly recommend that these

Sound field placement is crucial to the success of a spin bowler. To achieve this requires a healthy rapport between the captain and the bowler. There are also occasions when it requires the ability to compromise. Here, Mike Gatting and John Emburey are, I presume, figuring out the best possible options against India in 1986.

fielding positions are used very sparingly, if at all. In a shorter game, requiring quicker scoring, they become unnecessary, since the number of catches going there is probably exceeded by mishits into the outfield. Most importantly, there is a considerable risk of injury, especially for those not used to fielding so close. At least professionals are paid for standing there and should be insured against injury, but amateurs enjoying weekend cricket as a recreation might easily regret such bravado. These positions have, quite sensibly, been outlawed at youth level.

At the highest level these positions may also be over-employed, as Phil Edmonds suggests: 'I think we've become sterotyped as we look for bat/pad catches at the expense of everything else. Yet I don't really feel comfortable without a man at bat/pad; it almost becomes a sign of submission – admitting that the batsman is in charge. Wilf Slack at Middlesex sometimes says to me, "You're mad: why don't you settle back and let the batsman make the mistake?" Embers and I tend to overattack. It's part of my aggressive attitude. I do pick up a lot of wickets from catches at short-leg but certainly I should be more flexible.' So maybe it's worth both professional and amateur bowlers remembering that it is possible to bowl aggressively without fieldsmen huddled around the bat.

It is difficult to generalize about field placements; so much depends on the nature of the batsman. The basic principle is to place the fielders in a position where your opponent likes to hit the ball, assuming that the ball bowled is a good one. If by chance you have any fielders left over, stick them close to the wicket. If you haven't enough, maybe it is time for a rest.

With a little reluctance I have provided diagrams to show possible fields for spin bowlers (see pp.98–9).

A TURNING WICKET

Let us now suppose that the wicket is turning; this occurs less often since the full covering of wickets in England. Now spinners rely on dry, crumbling surfaces for spin rather than wet, drying wickets. On the old 'sticky wickets' the ball not only turned but bounced alarmingly; dry wickets don't necessarily provide bounce. If the wicket is turning the confident spinner starts to rub his hands together expectantly. Norman Gifford explains his reaction:

> 'When the wicket is in your favour you say, "My boy, I've waited a month to bowl on a surface like this. I'm the boss today." There is no need to seek much variety, but you have to find the right pace and still turn the ball. The quicker you can bowl it and still spin the ball the more problems you'll create. For instance, Derek Underwood was more lethal on bad wickets than Titmus or Illingworth.'

Edmonds and Pocock react in the same way, bowling slightly quicker, but Edmonds warns: 'Too often when spinners bowl quickly they forget to put body into their action; their arms come through quicker but lower, and their body doesn't come through in a vertical plane.' Just to confuse us, John Emburey tends to bowl slower on a turning wicket, even though he does so a little reluctantly. 'My strength is length and line, and once the ball starts to turn my line has to change. I often need to bowl a little fuller and therefore I bowl more bad balls on a turning

A rare sight in modern cricket: a 6 feet 6 inches West Indian bowling off spin. Roger Harper has been the lone spinner in the West Indian team for several years. His selection has been aided by his all round ability: his brilliant fielding and forthright batting. There is less scope for an out and out specialist in the modern game, unfortunately.

wicket than normal, which annoys me; I find the adjustment hard to make. In order to achieve a fuller length, I find I have to bowl slower.'

Turning wickets can seriously disrupt the batsman but they can also put pressure on the bowler, especially when the rest of the side can be overheard mumbling, 'Our spinner should get six wickets here.' As Pocock explains, 'If the ball is turning and bouncing, the gauntlet goes down; a professional batsman will usually react aggressively; modern players are not as adept as their predecessors at manipulating the ball, but they're much better at whacking boundaries.' It remains crucial to stop the batsman scoring. His patience will be stretched further by the knowledge that he's more likely to receive a brute of a delivery at any time.

Off spinners bowling at right handers will often bowl around the wicket if the ball is spinning, thereby increasing their chances of an LBW decision and preventing the batsman from indulging in one of the banes of the modern game – the thrusting of the left pad down the wicket with

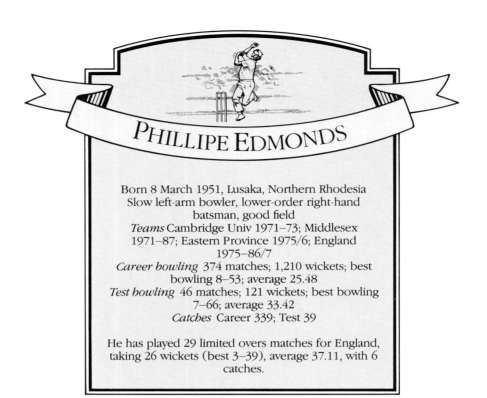

PHILLIPE EDMONDS

Born 8 March 1951, Lusaka, Northern Rhodesia
Slow left-arm bowler, lower-order right-hand
batsman, good field
Teams Cambridge Univ 1971–73; Middlesex
1971–87; Eastern Province 1975/6; England
1975–86/7
Career bowling 374 matches; 1,210 wickets; best
bowling 8–53; average 25.48
Test bowling 46 matches; 121 wickets; best bowling
7–66; average 33.42
Catches Career 339; Test 39

He has played 29 limited overs matches for England,
taking 26 wickets (best 3–39), average 37.11, with 6
catches.

the bat concealed behind the left knee, pretending to play a shot. Left-armers will invariably bowl around the wicket to right-hand batsmen. See diagram 2, pp.98–9 – but remember to stay flexible.

THE LIMITATIONS OF SPIN

Most spinners yearn to have a vicious bouncer in their armoury (Edmonds has one) so that they can relieve their frustration now and again. It is infuriating to see some slogger leap down the wicket and swing the perfect off spinner over mid-wicket. Spinners are a vulnerable breed; their best deliveries can be hit to the boundary, and it is important to come to terms with this sad fact. Pat Pocock has always been something of a philosopher:

> *'Over the last two decades I've dismissed Sobers, Kanhai, Richards and Lloyd but I've also been smashed around by tail-enders. I just try to bowl the ball where I want it to go, knowing full well that there's no guarantee that I'm going to get a wicket or avoid being hit for four. When the ball leaves my hand I must have done everything I can to ensure a successful trip. If a batsman has advanced and driven me I'm not unhappy, but if I've been cut or pulled I know I haven't given myself a chance and I'm annoyed.'*

Minor incidents can affect a spinner's confidence over a long period of time. In 1972 a 21-year-old Phil Edmonds played for Cambridge against Pakistan and bowled Zaheer

Abbas, a master of spin bowling, with a perfect arm ball. 'Ever since then he thought I could bowl, and for 15 years I knew he thought I could bowl. Psychologically I was always at ease bowling to Zaheer.' This is a luxury among spin bowlers. Similarly, there was a time when Emburey always troubled Gooch. When they played together for Western Province, however, Gooch spent hours facing Emburey in the nets and gradually ironed out his problems so that the balance was reversed. Now when they play in the same team, Emburey refuses to bowl off spinners in the nets to Gooch. Spinners have somehow to protect themselves and retain an inner confidence, even when the outlook is bleak.

Whenever Norman Gifford has been subjected to an onslaught by a batsman, he has consoled himself with the thought that just one batsman (Gary Sobers) has hit six sixes in an over (although Sobers has recently been joined by Ravi Shastri, who went berserk in Bombay). Such an indignity doesn't happen very often, and Gifford believes 'he'll succumb in the end'. However, he does recognize that it is harder for an emerging spinner; batsmen are more aggressive, and a young spinner is often regarded as light relief after a period of bombardment from the quick bowlers. At least Gifford can sometimes rely on his

Phil Edmonds has a classical left-arm spinner's action. His duels with Allan Border in recent Ashes' series have been fascinating to observe. Edmonds has certainly enjoyed the challenge and admits that he's more likely to bowl well against Border than Bruce Reid. Among the spinners that I've encountered, he has the best bouncer.

FIELD PLACINGS FOR SPIN BOWLERS

1. OFF SPINNER TO RIGHT-HAND BATSMAN – GOOD WICKET

Here are just a few of the endless possible variations.
1. If the batsman doesn't play the sweep shot, 5 might be brought up from the boundary to save the single.
2. If the batsman is a strong driver who is good at hitting 'over the top', 8 or 9 might be pushed back to the boundary.
3. If the wicket is very low-bouncing first slip may be superfluous since the ball won't carry and he may be better employed at silly point or on the leg side, provided the bowler is bowling at the stumps.
4. If the batsman is well set and scoring freely, 6 may be withdrawn to augment the leg-side fielders.

It is vital to remain alert and flexible, but don't move your fieldsmen every time the ball finds a gap.

Turning wicket

On a turning wicket we might have an extra boundary fielder at deep mid-wicket, since the batsman is more likely to go for the big hit. So 8 is moved to the boundary. No. 2 might go to silly point or leg slip: if the ball is turning it should be difficult for the batsman to cut the ball into that area. The bowler should pitch the ball so that it hits the stumps.

2. LEFT-ARM SPINNER TO RIGHT-HAND BATSMAN – GOOD WICKET

This field assumes that the bowler is aiming to pitch just outside off stump in order to hit it.
1. If the batsman is tentative and just prodding forward, 3 might go to silly point; or, if he is mis-timing his drives, 3 might move to short extra cover.
2. If the batsman doesn't sweep, 6 could save the single.
3. If the batsman is in control, 7 might augment the off side field and 5 may go to long-off.

It is always a ticklish dilemma deciding when to position a long-off or long-on. Initially, spinners may be pleased that a batsman hits over the top: a mis-timed drive to mid-on/off is a distinct possibility. However, if the batsman has hit the ball convincingly over your head two or three times, it is wise to put a fielder back as a deterrent. This move will stop most batsmen from persisting with the lofted drive.

Turning wicket

On a turning wicket, the likes of Underwood would aim to pitch the ball on middle/leg stump allowing it to turn and hit off stump. No. 3 might move into the gully and 8 to silly point. This leaves a large gap at mid-wicket; however, driving through that area should be dangerous and encouraged.

3. OFF SPINNER TO RIGHT-HAND BATSMAN – ONE-DAY GAME

The aim for the bowler is to make the batsman hit the ball on the leg side to 4, 5, 6 and 7 who, ideally, should be the best fielders. He should aim for middle/leg stump.

The batsman may step outside leg stump in order to hit through the sparsely guarded off side. The bowler now has two options: either to continue bowling straight in the hope that the batsman is not capable of concocting a cover drive on the move, or the usual course, which is to follow the batsman as he moves so that the ball lands close to his left foot, thereby allowing him no room to swing the bat.

Mid-off and mid-on can be shuffled to the boundary, depending on the situation and the batsman's capabilities. If 4 is on the edge, 5 should move squarer. It's worth keeping mid-off and mid-on in as long as possible, preventing the single and improving the chances of taking a wicket from a mis-timed lofted drive.

4. LEFT-ARM SPINNER TO RIGHT-HAND BATSMAN – ONE-DAY GAME

This is a commonly used field for slow left armers. The emphasis here is on the leg side, unlike three-day cricket, demanding the bowler to aim for middle stump. Deep mid-wicket and mid-off can either save the single or the boundary. Edmonds sometimes reverts to the more traditional off side attack by moving 9 to the off side.

5. LEG SPINNER TO RIGHT-HAND BATSMAN

Rather than bowl on or outside off stump, Holland prefers to pitch the ball on middle and leg stump, encouraging the batsman to drive through the leg side against the spin. If the ball is turning the batsman is likely to mis-time his drive or get a leading edge, providing catching opportunities for the ring of fieldsmen 20 yards from the bat. Holland tempts the batsman to drive when the ball is not full enough, while he alternates between his stock ball (the leg break), his 45° leg break, his top spinner and his googly which, he admits, does not spin a great deal.

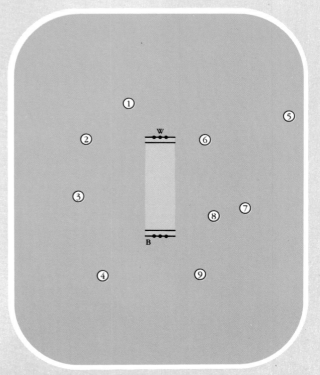

Diagram 1 Key: 1, first slip; 2, cover point; 3, extra cover; 4, mid-off; 5, deep backward square-leg; 6, forward short leg; 7, mid-wicket; 8, short mid-wicket; 9, mid-on.

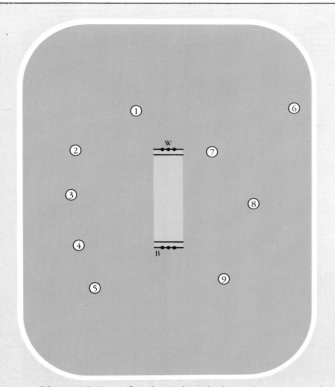

Diagram 2 Key: 1, first slip; 2, short third man; 3, cover point; 4, extra cover; 5, mid-off; 6, deep backward square-leg; 7, forward short-leg; 8, mid-wicket; 9, mid-on.

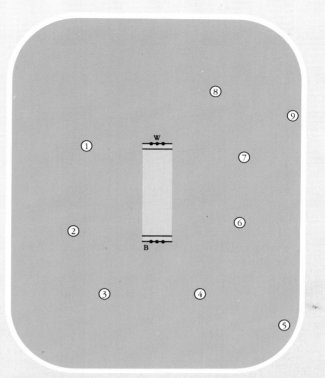

Diagram 3 Key: 1, point; 2, extra cover; 3, mid-off; 4, mid-on; 5, deep mid-wicket; 6, mid-wicket; 7, square leg; 8, short fine leg; 9, deep backward square-leg.

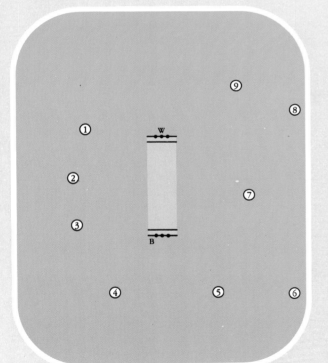

Diagram 4 Key: 1, short third man; 2, cover point; 3, extra cover; 4, mid-off; 5, mid-on; 6, deep mid-wicket; 7, mid-wicket; 8, deep backward square-leg; 9, short fine leg.

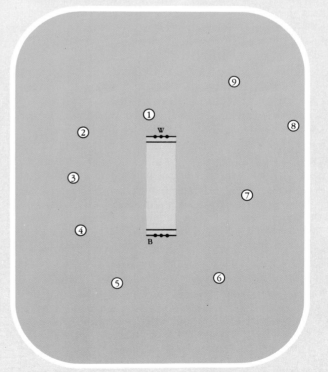

Diagram 5 Key: 1, first slip; 2, short third man; 3, cover point; 4, extra cover; 5, mid-off; 6, mid-on; 7, mid-wicket; 8, deep square-leg; 9, short fine leg.

reputation and longevity to command a little respect. When he began his career in the early Sixties, few batsmen would try to hit aerially, but now good players with their Magnums, Jumbos or Giants try to spread the field immediately. This change in approach has been caused mainly by the advent of limited overs cricket, which has compelled batsmen to discover and attempt new shots but has had a detrimental effect on developing spinners. The tendency is for them to bowl with a very flat trajectory to a negative leg-side line and to drop their arms. Then it becomes very difficult to readjust to 'proper' cricket.

LIMITED OVERS MATCHES

Nonetheless, spinners can be most effective in limited overs cricket, for two reasons. First, they should be more accurate than the faster bowlers: secondly, since they bowl slower they demand that the batsman takes the initiative, and deflections are no longer profitable. So a spinner can pose many problems, especially if the batsman is tentative or the situation demands a no-risk policy from the batting side. If, however, the batsmen are attacking, the spinner must at least try to dictate to which area of the ground they will hit the ball and put plenty of fielders there.

At the end of an innings, with batsmen swinging merrily, most spinners try to bowl a fuller length to prevent the batsman from getting enough leverage to swing the ball out of the ground. Emburey often ends up bowling fast yorkers. At this stage bowling spin becomes unrecognizable from the traditional, subtle arts of three, four or five day cricket and a youngster's action and confidence can be easily damaged.

All the best spinners have succeeded in limited overs cricket. For as long as possible in each spell they stick to the fundamentals they practise in three-day cricket, but always ensuring that they give the batsman no room to swing the bat. Variety is still important – perhaps even more so, for it is much easier for a batsman to premeditate a shot if he knows where and when the ball will land.

For Norman Gifford, bowling in one-day cricket came as a fresh challenge midway through his career and, of course, he enjoys it. So maybe those of us who are younger should do the same. The duel between batsman and bowler is more intense, less subtle but equally satisfying when won. See diagrams 3 and 4, pp.98–9.

Sivaramakrishnan displays some magic even before he starts his approach to the wicket. If it's his day he can be brilliant; if not, very expensive – such uncertainty poses a common dilemma for leg spinners and captains alike.

THE LEG SPINNER

Leg spinners need special attention: they are now regarded as freaks and, sadly, are almost extinct. There are now no serious leg spinners in England (I don't think Kim Barnett would be offended to read that). Neither the West Indies nor New Zealand has played one for years. Pakistan have Abdul Qadir and India occasionally play Sivaramakrishnan, if only to keep visiting commentators on their mettle. In Australia, the land of O'Reilly, Grimmett and Benaud, there were just three playing State cricket during the 1986/7 season.

I spoke to one of them; Bob Holland, of New South Wales and Australia, whose career has been suitably freakish. Holland did not play for New South Wales until the age of 32 and he was 38 when he embarked on his first overseas tour (to England in 1985). Living outside Sydney (in Newcastle) may have restricted his opportunities, but he gained valuable first class experience in those early years playing several representative games for Northern New South Wales, beginning with a fixture against M.J.K. Smith's 1965 tourists.

He recalls spending hours as a child throwing a cricket ball from the back of his hand against a brick wall,

Holland to Botham – a duel well worth watching. Both had their victories. Holland prefers to bowl to batsmen who attack him, which may account for his success against the West Indians.

imparting spin to make it deviate on its return. By the age of 16 he was in his first grade side in Newcastle as a batsman who sometimes bowled wrist spin. Even the early Sixties could be a frustrating time for a young leg spinner waiting for a chance to bowl, constantly eyeing the captain as the opposition score rose, becoming bemused that he should be ignored for so long. Finally he might be granted four overs; they might cost 25 runs and bring no wickets, justifying his captain's hesitancy. But increasingly these overs were more likely to produce wickets.

In fact, sheer volume of wickets plus success in his few representative games took him into the State side and on 2 January 1985 the Australian public found an unlikely hero in him when, on a turning wicket at Sydney, he captured 10 wickets in a Test match, inflicting a rare defeat upon the West Indies and producing a rare victory for Australia. The pundits, especially Richie Benaud, were delighted. Yet a couple of years later no new leg spinners are on the horizon. Why? Holland gives us his opinion:

'This is the age of "containment cricket". They want all the bowlers to bowl at 2½ runs per over; no one is prepared to experiment. Bowling that doesn't fit into a one-day pattern is viewed with great suspicion. Also, young people now have so many other things to do; they may like cricket, but they don't spend as much time practising, since there are so many distractions. Leg spin, being the most difficult type of bowling, needs the most practice. It's easier to become a medium pacer.'

And yet the delight at witnessing a batsman being completely outwitted by your googly or leg spinner must compensate for all that hard work. The complete leg spinner has more options available than any other type of bowler. His stock ball is the leg break, which moves from leg to off after pitching. The ball is gripped in the hand with the third finger down the seam. As the ball is released the wrist is turned sharply and the hand is brought down the inside of the ball. At the point of release (at least in Holland's case) the back of the hand faces the bowler. Bob Holland can determine the amount of spin he imparts. He has a second leg spinner at his command, which spins less but dips in the air and swings in a little; when he bowls this type of ball, the back of his hand is at 45° rather than facing him directly.

The googly or 'wrong un' should look like a leg break, but spin in the opposite direction. This delivery is made with the same grip, the only difference coming at the release point when the wrist is rolled over so that the ball comes out of the back of the hand, which is now facing the batsman.

For those unaccustomed to leg spin, it's hard to tell the difference. In grade cricket in Newcastle, Holland's opponents began to pick out his googly because it became known that his little finger stuck out (like Dame Edna drinking a cup of tea) as he was gripping the ball. Once

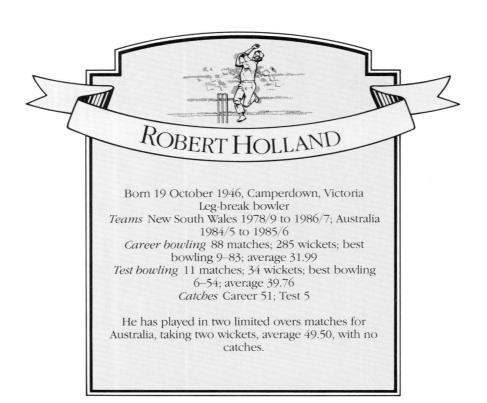

ROBERT HOLLAND

Born 19 October 1946, Camperdown, Victoria
Leg-break bowler
Teams New South Wales 1978/9 to 1986/7; Australia
1984/5 to 1985/6
Career bowling 88 matches; 285 wickets; best
bowling 9–83; average 31.99
Test bowling 11 matches; 34 wickets; best bowling
6–54; average 39.76
Catches Career 51; Test 5

He has played in two limited overs matches for
Australia, taking two wickets, average 49.50, with no
catches.

Holland realized that the code was being cracked, he naturally ensured that his little finger was sticking out when he bowled his leg breaks as well.

The top spinner should dip in its flight, bounce more and fizz through: this is bowled by rolling the wrist over the ball and imparting overspin, making the ball hurry on straight.

The 'flipper', which was an invaluable part of Grimmett's and Benaud's armoury, is a ball that arrives before the batsman expects it. Again, the action should resemble a leg break, but the ball is squeezed out of the hand in a variety of individually devised ways. Apparently Grimmett's flipper snapped out of his hand with a fearful crack, which gave the game away until he started clicking the fingers of his left hand when bowling other deliveries.

These definitions may be a little bewildering in print. It is much easier for a prospective wrist spinner to take a ball and experiment: you may be surprised at the variations that occur.

Bob Holland has a refreshingly old-fashioned approach to spinning. He bowls slower than most and he doesn't like having many close fielders in front of the bat since he recognizes that a) it is important to tie the batsman down and b) it is more difficult to bowl leg spinners accurately. He wants the batsman to attack him and his field is set accordingly; see diagram 5, pp.98–9. Of course some

Bob Holland gives us a good example of the wrist spinners action at Trent Bridge in 1985.

Who knows whether he'll deliver a leg spinner, top spinner or googly?

batsman, such as Botham, do not need a great deal of encouragement to drive. Holland has dismissed him several times, but he's also been thumped by him. How does he react when he's in the firing line?

'I have a system which sometimes I remember to use and sometimes, in the heat of the moment, I don't. If I'm in trouble, I always try to think that there's no batsman at the other end. So I don't look up at the batsman, but fix my eyes at a spot on the wicket and aim for it. If I hit that spot and the batsman still smashes the ball, I don't feel too bad.'

Not all leg spinners are so phlegmatic or philosophical. Of the current leg spinners, Abdul Qadir from Karachi is the most gifted. Unlike Holland, he is overtly full of aggression, happy only if he has a cluster of fieldsmen around the bat; he wants a wicket every ball. Temperamentally, Holland operates like a finger spinner, say John Emburey, while Qadir has more in common with Freddie Trueman.

It would be a tragedy if the leg spinner disappeared from the scene altogether. I'm sure that if a good one – like Qadir – were to play a season's County cricket he would be successful, if only because there's a rapidly diminishing number of batsmen who have any experience against leg spin. The return of the leg spinner would certainly enliven the English season. Whoever is reading this particular section must be both remarkably dedicated and sufficiently off beat to be a wrist spinner. Put the book down and start practising.

14   MILDURA

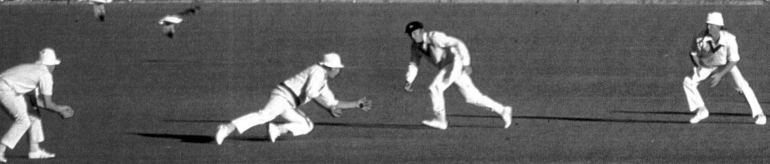

BENSON and HEDGES

IN THE FIELD

'...*you must assume that every ball is coming to you.*'

GRAEME FOWLER

The Australians in the field, alert and aggressive – which is hardly surprising as this is the Centenary Test, Melbourne, 1977.

*C*ricketers spend more of their lives fielding than either batting or bowling, yet it is only during the last two decades, with the advent of so much limited overs cricket, that teams have paid much attention to this aspect of the game. As a result, the overall standard of fielding in first class cricket has undoubtedly improved. Between the wars it would have been remarkable to see a fieldsman actually dive in an attempt to stop the ball, whereas it is now commonplace; and I doubt whether even Jardine's sides spent 15 minutes together each morning practising their fielding. That, however, is the pattern for international sides today.

Such an approach makes good sense. For me, the most exciting and uplifting experience in cricket (maybe because it doesn't happen very often) is pulling off a difficult catch and observing the reaction of those around – the surprise of team-mates, the batsman's sense of betrayal and the sheer delight of the bowler. A brilliant catch or run out can transform the mood of a fielding side in a split second.

Conversely, dropping a catch is the worst feeling in cricket. There is nowhere to hide. At least if a batsman has made a crass error he is compelled to leave the arena. An erring fieldsman doesn't have that luxury, though he may suffer the indignity of being moved ostentatiously from second slip to deep third man, where at Eastbourne he might hear whispers from the deckchairs or, at Melbourne, constant ridicule and piercing abuse from Bay 13.

It is at times like these that the virtues of regular, conscientious practice are most readily recognized. Daryl Foster, coach of Western Australia, believes that 'if you take a thousand catches in practice you're more likely to catch the thousand-and-first, whether at practice or in a game'. Daryl has been responsible for sending WA sides out into the field for the last 12 years and has hit catches to the likes of Ross Edwards, Ken McEwan, Dennis Lillee, Kim Hughes and Graeme Wood. During this period WA won the Sheffield Shield six times.

Daryl is a rare breed among coaches involved at the highest level since he has never played first class cricket (though he had a distinguished career at grade level in Melbourne and Perth). I wondered whether this lack of first class experience had made it more difficult for him to be accepted. He answered, 'It hasn't been a problem with the players; when you are working closely with a side you either win or lose their confidence by what you say and do,

not through your previous cricketing prowess. However, it is often a problem for the administrators, who find it hard to understand that anyone other than a first class cricketer can become a first class coach.'

In English soccer it has often been shown that the best players rarely become the best managers, while average players often become excellent coaches. The same, I'm certain, applies in cricket. Foster's lack of top class experience has one definite advantage for all concerned; he's not in a position to irritate his players with constant references to 'the good old days when we played the game properly'. His profession has also helped him; he is currently Head of the PE Department of the University of Western Australia. His own knowledge, along with easy access to physiologists and sports psychologists, has helped him in his preparation of training routines for the State side. In turn, the State players readily acknowledge that they have benefited from their coach; this is a surprisingly rare state of affairs among first class cricketers.

Fielding can – mistakenly – be regarded as an interlude between batting; a time to rest and relax while the bowlers get on with their job. In reality, it requires a tougher mental approach than the other two disciplines, since a fieldsman's opportunity to contribute can be so sporadic. First slip can spend five and a half hours standing next to the wicketkeeper without touching the ball in earnest; yet, when that snick finally comes at 5.30 pm, he is expected to catch it. That sort of concentration is harder to achieve than when you are batting or bowling, when there is less scope for the mind to wander.

Foster confirms what Rod Marsh says about concentration. 'I don't think anyone can concentrate absolutely for six hours each day. Cricket should be played a ball at a time and players have to train themselves to focus in on a small event, to give it their best attention and then to defocus for a while.'

Top class fieldsmen do this automatically. Bobby Simpson, a brilliant first slip for Australia, waited until the very last moment before the bowler delivered the ball before taking up his catching position. Botham does the same, minimizing that period of intense concentration. If Concorde, the Red Arrows or a kingfisher are flying overhead, it is ridiculous to become agitated by their presence because of a fear of being distracted by them. It is much better to enjoy their presence and to come to terms with it before refocusing on the bowler and the ball.

THE FIELDING POSITIONS

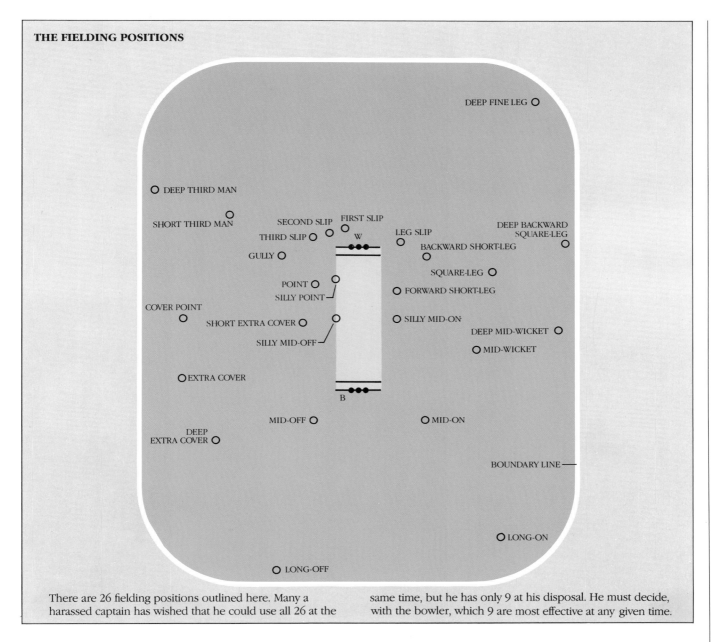

DEEP FINE LEG ○

○ DEEP THIRD MAN

SHORT THIRD MAN ○   SECOND SLIP FIRST SLIP

THIRD SLIP ○ ○ ○ LEG SLIP   DEEP BACKWARD
W   SQUARE-LEG

GULLY ○   ○ BACKWARD SHORT-LEG ○

POINT ○ ○   SQUARE-LEG ○
SILLY POINT ⌐

COVER POINT   ○ FORWARD SHORT-LEG
○

SHORT EXTRA COVER ○ ○ ○ SILLY MID-ON
SILLY MID-OFF ⌐   DEEP MID-WICKET ○

○ EXTRA COVER   ○ MID-WICKET

B

MID-OFF ○   ○ MID-ON

DEEP
EXTRA COVER ○

BOUNDARY LINE —

○ LONG-ON

○ LONG-OFF

There are 26 fielding positions outlined here. Many a harassed captain has wished that he could use all 26 at the same time, but he has only 9 at his disposal. He must decide, with the bowler, which 9 are most effective at any given time.

I think that I dread dropping a catch more than anything else on a cricket field. This is a pity, as Foster points out that 'fear and anxiety often lead to failure'. Botham's greatest asset as a cricketer has been that he doesn't fear failure. In Marsh and Lillee, Foster has witnessed players who instinctively react in a positive way to any challenge; they are naturally competitive and confident. Others have to try to acquire or improve upon these qualities.

Foster believes that it is crucial how each player talks to himself. 'For instance, after a bad misfield, a player can react in two ways – positively: "That wasn't like me, next time I'll pick it up cleanly and hit the stumps" – or negatively: "There I go again, misfielding. What an idiot; I always do that". Since the mind doesn't know the difference between what is actually happening and what it perceives is happening, how we talk to ourselves in the field is most important. By talking to ourselves positively and having a clear picture in our minds of what we want to achieve, we can improve our performances dramatically.' Naturally this applies to fielding, batting and bowling.

Each side should try to develop specialist fielders, while recognizing that with so much one-day cricket everyone must be able to field everywhere. It must have come as a real shock to Phil Sharpe, a master first slip for Yorkshire who began his career in the Fifties, to suddenly have to desert his post in a John Player League game at the end of the Sixties. Still, different positions require different attributes. Let me try to outline them.

Left *A brilliant catch by Mike Brearley at first slip, requiring agility and superb reflexes. Derek Underwood is about to celebrate. Such a catch can lift the entire fielding side and change the tenor of a game; Centenary Test, Melbourne, 1977.*

Above *John Emburey provides an excellent example of how to take an outfield catch. He is well balanced, his head is still with eyes on the ball and his hands are in the right place; England v Western Australia County XI at Kalgoorli, November 1986.*

First slip

He must have tremendous powers of concentration and sharp reflexes; like the wicketkeeper, he has to expect every ball, yet he might receive only one or two each day. With weight slightly forwards, hands at the ready near the ground, he should watch the ball out of the bowler's hand and, like all good catchers, wait for it rather than snatch. It is a mentally rather than physically demanding position, and it has great compensations. It is the best place (apart from a deck chair) from which to watch the game, ideal for captains, provided they can catch – Brearley, Gatting, Lloyd, Coney have all fielded in the slips. It's best to have a specialist first slip so that he can build up an understanding with the wicketkeeper regarding positioning. It also helps if they like one another.

Ian Botham about to catch Larry Gomes to provide Richard Ellison with his first Test wicket. Botham stands closer than most second slips, which is probably why the ball is still at head height. He prefers to risk dropping the ball than seeing it bounce in front of him. The Oval, 1984.

Second slip

A high proportion of slip catches end up here. Most players watch the bat, but some of the finest, like Graham Roope of Surrey and England and Ian Botham, watch the ball from the bowler's hand. Botham stands much closer than the rest since 'as a bowler there's nothing more frustrating than seeing the ball pitch short of the fieldsman. Also, you're cutting down the angle: a ball that you might dive for normally will be nearer your body if you are two yards closer'. However, you need superb reflexes to field as close as Botham and his position often disrupts the alignment of the rest of the slip cordon. Also his habit of keeping his hands on his knees at all times is not recommended for lesser players.

Third and fourth slip

They invariably watch the bat; these are less likely to be specialist fieldsmen since three or four slips are seldom maintained for the whole day – unless you happen to be playing for the West Indies.

Gully

This is frequently the home of a senior man, with reflexes intact; he is still mobile, though not necessarily over long distances. Phil Edmonds often patrols there for England; Joel Garner for the West Indies. Years ago, Bill Alley, well into his forties, stood there for Somerset and caught anything within reach, but he was seldom seen sprinting towards third man to retrieve edges.

Garner obeys the normal rules for a close fieldsman. He 'switches on' when the bowler is about three strides from delivering, then focuses on the bat and stays low until the shot is completed. Curiously, he finds concentration easier when he's bowling at the other end; his mind is less likely to wander from the game as he's probing for weaknesses, while his body feels more supple and agile.

Edmonds admits that he has to work hard to retain concentration: 'I've developed a routine for the gully: I draw a 6-yard box like a goalkeeper and that is my box. Anything in there I'm going to catch, so when the bowler runs up I focus on the area of grass between myself and my line. I get down and I always inhale as the ball is being released so that my weight is forward. Then I'm ready.'

The depth of the gully fieldsman is dependent upon who is batting and whether he is attacking or defending. A sensible gully will probably stand a little deeper when Gordon Greenidge is on strike rather than Jim Griffiths.

Short-leg/silly point

If the gully is often the preserve of the elder statesman, forward short-leg and silly point are sometimes the lot of the younger members of the team. There's no logical reason for this – except that there are rarely many volunteers for these positions. For a fielder perched precariously 5 feet from the bat, an element of danger is inevitably introduced. As a slow bowler I've felt admiration and gratitude for these fearless close fielders: I've even bought one of my short-legs a pair of shin pads for his birthday – probably an unwitting attempt to ease my conscience.

Outside first class cricket, these positions should be employed very sparingly and never in youth cricket. At least professionals, who field there regularly, learn safety techniques which the more occasional cricketer might not pick up in time. At silly point the most vulnerable areas are the lower leg and ankles; hence an experienced man like David Gower can anticipate the batsman's shot and, timing his jump to perfection, evade the ball; this is also very photogenic.

By contrast, forward short-leg, if he wants to take evasive action from a long hop, turns his back and curls up to reduce the target area. Such men need to be brave and none was braver than Brian Close, who, by all accounts, never took evasive action at all. This well-worn story,

David Gower is excellent at silly point; he's also very good at taking evasive action, as this photograph demonstrates. The most vulnerable areas are the ankles and shins, which David

has gracefull removed from the firing line. The keeper is Bruce French, the batsman Azharuddin. The bowler would probably prefer to remain anonymous.

apparently true, now has to be retold just in case someone missed it. Close, while fielding short-leg, was hit on the side of the head and the ball ricocheted to gully who caught it, thereby dismissing the batsman. Amid the celebrations one of the more naïve youngsters in the side, who was concerned about Close's well being, asked him what would have happened if the ball had hit him straight between the eyes – 'He'd have been caught at cover point, lad'.

Apart from bravery and the ability to keep moving forward when the sensible thing to do is to retreat, these fieldsmen also need sharp reflexes and a devotion to duty.

Cover/mid-wicket

Cover has always been regarded as the glamour position in the outfield. I expect that Roy of the Rovers, when playing for Melchester C.C. in the off season, fielded at cover: and I know that Colin Bland did so for South Africa, Paul Sheahan for Australia and, in his youth, Clive Lloyd for the West Indies. A good cover fieldsman is quick off the mark

in any direction; he is sufficiently well balanced and coordinated to pick up the ball easily, and he can throw swiftly and accurately. It is a prime area for run outs from direct hits; David Gower has become a master of the underarm flick from close range, while the likes of Bland, Lloyd and Richards developed outstanding accuracy from longer, harder throws.

Graeme Fowler of Lancashire and England, since he wisely forsook wicketkeeping, has spent most of his career in the covers. He reckons that ideally the cover should be right handed and the mid-wicket left handed since that makes it easier to swoop on pushes wide of mid-off and mid-on with the throwing arm (thereby deterring a run or causing a run out).

The cover fieldsman should stand as deep as possible, while still being able to save the single; he should adjust according to the pace of the outfield, the speed of the batsmen between the wickets and even the state of the game. If the batsmen are struggling for runs against quality

bowling they are more likely to attempt quick singles, so cover/mid-wicket might be a little closer. If they're smashing boundaries, it's wiser to retreat a little.

Outfielders always walk in with the bowler so that they have enough momentum to move quickly in any direction. Derek Randall might hop, skip and jump for about 25 yards before the ball is bowled, whereas Gower is more likely to take three steps. Fowler finds that when the batsman hits the ball both his feet are planted on the ground so that he can push off either way. Over the years his anticipation has been improved by his own early warning system. From the corner of his eye, he picks up the length of the delivery to establish whether it's likely to be cut or driven and he studies how the batsman is shaping to play his shot. This gives him a better idea of where the ball is going, though it is not a foolproof system as he can't guarantee that the batsman is going to middle the ball.

Fowler, like all good covers, can sense the possibility of a run out. Now is the time to forsake the golden rule 'Two

hands to the ball' in the interests of speed. He tries to pick the ball up by his right foot and throw it after just one stride, while pointing at his target with his front (left) arm. The supernaturals like Lloyd in his youth and Roger Harper today can somehow throw it accurately without taking a step at all. That seems to be beyond most of us.

Mid-off/mid-on

These positions have been much maligned over the years. Ranji wrote that 'mid-on is perhaps the best place to put a duffer, if you are unfortunate enough to have one'. Ever since then the third man/mid-on trail has been reserved for the dozy, the unreliable and the unathletic. Now, for some reason I've had considerable experience at mid-on and I regard it as a very tricky position. Indeed, when I'm bowling I like to ensure that I have one of my better fielders at mid-on since to an off spinner he's likely to be busy and to receive catches.

In these positions it is particularly hard to judge the pace of the ball and whether it has been hit cleanly; this becomes vital when the ball is in the air. Swirling mishits often end up in this area, particularly in the latter part of a one-day innings, so I would recommend that captains stick reliable catchers there.

Mid-off/on are in a good position to chat to the bowler and for this reason captains who can't catch at slip often

Above Chris Smith, like most forward short-legs, wears a helmet. The only disadvantage is that if the ball rebounds off the helmet and is caught, the catch doesn't count. Presumably, this is the reason why Brian Close chose never to wear one. The batsman is Martin Crowe; Lord's 1983.

Right Even the best can drop them. After a mistake the fieldsman should still want the ball to come to him, preferably in the air; not many of us do, though. England v India, Lord's, June 1986.

Above *Miller catches Thomson and England win by 2 runs. Melbourne, 1982.*

field there. A few words of encouragement to the bowler are seldom wasted; at the very least, try to avoid emitting a series of expletives when another long hop has been crashed to the boundary.

Long-leg

This is the traditional resting place of the fast bowler; in the old days he might be able to smuggle a rejuvenating pint of best bitter from an understanding spectator down at long-leg. In this scientific modern era probably the best he can hope for is a glass of staminade from the twelfth man. Long-leg should suit a strong fast bowler. Ideally, he is quick across the grass and eager to attack the ball with a strong arm. Skied catches from mishooks occasionally come to long-leg so don't relax too much, especially if Botham is bowling the other end.

Third man

The great thing about fielding third man is that catches hardly ever get there. Just occasionally a wild slash outside the off stump from a fast delivery will reach an astounded third man; but this is a freakish shot and you will have every right to feel victimized if it happens to you. A good long-leg will find third man a doddle.

However this position, like all the others, is transformed when the match is a limited overs contest. Batsmen will be scurrying down the wickets to try to put pressure on the third man to concede two runs. This is when the third man requires all the attributes of the complete boundary fielder.

Boundary fielders

These are most prevalent in limited overs matches when captains usually avoid putting me on the boundary, so I've interrogated Graeme Fowler and asked him for his opinion. What are the requirements?

'Usually there will be someone in front of you (eg a short mid-wicket) but you must assume that every ball is coming to you. This means making a lot of dummy runs. When the ball does defeat the infield, the captain wants you to ensure that there's no second run, so you must attack the ball by running towards it in a straight line and you throw it as quickly as possible. It's better to bounce the ball to the wicketkeeper quickly, thereby stopping the batsmen running, rather than taking your time and meticulously producing the

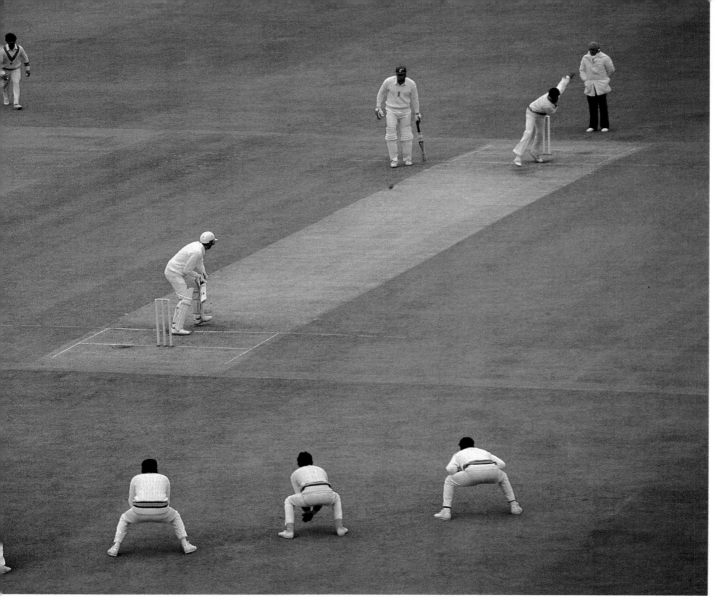

perfect throw which takes so long to arrive that the batsmen have run two anyway.

'As far as throwing technique is concerned, I advocate throwing from over the top of the shoulder – a little like a tennis serve. The front arm should be high, with the throwing arm starting from well behind the body. Then transfer the weight from back to front foot as you let go of the ball and follow through just like a bowler.

'When catching, I like to present the largest possible area to the ball with my hands, whether I'm catching with my fingers pointing to the sky (Australian style) or whether they're directed at the ground: then I'll gently absorb the shock of the ball. Ideally I'll be stationary, but this doesn't happen often in a match. Self confidence is important and that can be developed by regular practice. I try to put myself under pressure when practising. Some people will ignore catches if they are more than 5 yards away. I go for everything, even if it does mean dirtying my tracksuit.'

A good example of an eager and well placed slip cordon awaiting an outside edge from John Emburey's bat. The slip fielders should be as far apart as possible while allowing nothing to pass between them. Note that the Indian fielders are all squatting close to the ground. It's much easier to come up than go down. Lord's, June 1986.

PRACTISING SKILLS

Which takes us back to Daryl Foster and the importance of practising fielding skills. He does not have much time for intricate, sophisticated fielding routines which require a degree in geography or mathematics to complete. He is more concerned that everyone is kept busy and that the available time is used as efficiently as possible. Groups of four and five are ideal, since 1:5 is the perfect interval training ratio so that fielding and fitness are improved simultaneously. Slip catchers will use the nicking technique described in Chapter 1 and outfielders will practise every possible type of catch – skiers, skimmers and those you can't quite reach.

Foster thinks that cricketers can learn a great deal from other sports, and as a result Western Australia were one of the first sides to use baseball gloves as part of their practice. He says,

'It alarmed me that so many guys couldn't throw in from the boundary because of shoulder injuries. By constantly throwing the ball into your partner's glove at various distances, you keep your shoulder in

A STANDARD ONE-DAY FIELD IN THE MIDDLE OF AN INNINGS

There are endless permutations, but in one-day cricket at County or international level, four fielders must stay within the inner ring. The bowler should be aiming to hit off stump, since the majority of his fielders are on the off side.

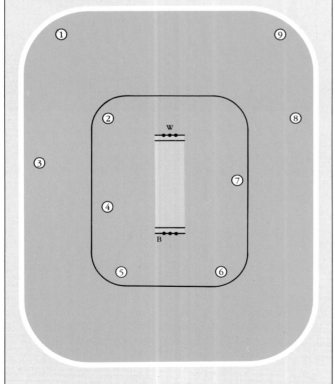

Key: 1, third man; 2, cover point; 3, deep cover; 4, extra cover; 5, mid-off; 6, mid-on; 7, mid-wicket; 8, deep backward square-leg; 9, long leg.

reasonable nick and you can develop greater power and accuracy. Even some first class players have poor throwing actions which put strain upon elbow and shoulder joints, so we try to teach them to throw properly in the off season.'

To confirm Foster's point, I noticed that by the end of England's triumphant tour of Australia in 1986/7 five of the side which won the one-day series had 'lost' their throwing arms. As a result Mike Gatting, the captain, was often compelled to lead the side from the boundary.

The practice becomes more purposeful using Foster's routine with baseball gloves since everyone is working in pairs; once the arms have been loosened a variety of fielding exercises can be set up. Certainly this is more efficient than having one wicketkeeper, one batter and nine dawdling fieldsmen.

England's Derek Randall about to be run out by Sikander Bakht of Pakistan. This is the most demoralizing and embarrassing way for a batsman to be dismissed. Ironically, Derek Randall was fast and could run like a gazelle, but not always in the right direction. 1982.

Having expressed a certain disdain for most artificial fielding exercises, let me just add two simple ones to those already mentioned in 'Preparing for the Season'. The first stems from baseball, and should improve short distance throwing.

Four stumps are placed in a square, like baseball bases, approximately 25 yards apart. At each stump is a fieldsman. While one player sprints around the square once, the fielders have to throw a ball from stump to stump around the square twice. The runner and the ball should arrive home at about the same time – and then some lively arguments begin.

The second exercise should help throwing in a run out situation. A wicketkeeper stands behind one stump, with the other stump approximately 12 yards away. While a batsman sprints from the first stump to the second and back again, the ball is rolled out to a fielder about 30–40 yards from the keeper. The fielder has to return it to the keeper quickly enough to run the batsman out. More arguments. Both exercises probably require neutral umpires.

Limited overs cricket now provides a wonderful stage for the gifted fielder and, unfortunately, a formidable obstacle course for the less gifted among us – so while some of you might strive to emulate Derek Randall or Viv Richards, those of us blessed with less speed and slower reactions should practise hard so that at the very least we can become 'reliable'. After all, we can't field third man all our lives.

THE
KEEPER

'I made it very plain to my fielders that I set the standard and if any of them didn't reach it I let them know I wasn't happy about it.'

ROD MARSH

Greig caught Marsh, bowled Gilmour; Prudential World Cup, 1975.

'All the mistakes of the wicketkeeper and some not perpetrated by him are mercilessly chalked up by the recording angels in the Press Box.' That comment might have been uttered by Rod Marsh after his first Test appearance at the Gabba in 1970/1, when he dropped four tricky chances and was immediately dubbed 'Iron Gloves' by the media. In fact it was good old Ranji again. Whether the year is 1896 or 1986 the wicketkeeper's job is a thankless one. As with a goalkeeper, his game is a closed book to the other 10 players, who often fail to appreciate the skills involved, but who are quick to complain when a catch or a stumping goes astray. That's why you can often spot opposition wicketkeepers chatting to one another and comparing notes at the end of the day; nobody else understands the special demands of their role.

Rod Marsh started keeping wicket at the age of eight for his local U/16B team. Even then he liked to be involved in the game all the time: in fact, there were so many pre-teenage kids in the side that they were known as 'the mosquito fleet'. By the age of 12 he was keeping in a fourth grade side in Perth and by 16 he was in the A grade team as a batsman, deputizing for State keeper Gordon Becker when he was absent. He spent hours at the Western Australia Cricket Association in Perth; then, as now, he observed the wicketkeeper first and the game afterwards. He can recall being impressed by Godfrey Evans in 1958/9,

but his greatest inspiration was Wally Grout, Australia's keeper from 1958 to 1965.

He made his debut for Western Australia in 1968/9 – purely as a batsman – against the West Indies, and scored 0 in his first innings and 100 in his second. In his next match he scored 0 again but wasn't too worried, as he confidently assumed that he would make another hundred in the second innings; in fact, he made 22. The following year he kept for Western Australia and after notable performances with gloves and bat on an early Eastern States tour in 1970 he was selected for his first Test Match. Being dubbed 'Iron Gloves' may have briefly dented his confidence but it also doubled his determination to succeed and he started training 'as never before'. An excellent tour of England in 1972 established him as Australia's No. 1 keeper, and from then on he did not miss a Test match, apart from during the Packer interlude, until his retirement in 1984.

Marsh is remembered by many as being part of that formidable triumvirate of Ian Chappell, Lillee and Marsh – the epitome of the brash, rough, tough, beer-swilling Aussie. However, those who have met him or played against him soon realize that this is only a fraction of the truth. Indeed, Mike Brearley in *The Art of Captaincy* acknowledges this when assessing recent Australian captains.

BASIC STANCE

Keith Andrew, who describes the technical points shown in the artwork throughout the book, is particularly well qualified to do so in this chapter. In the Fifties and Sixties he was universally regarded as one of England's finest keepers.

The basic stance is a comfortable squatting position with the weight on the balls of the feet. The eyes are level and looking directly ahead. The hands are together with the palms facing outwards, towards the bowler, and the backs of the gloves touching the ground.

TAKING ON THE OFF SIDE

Good stance – ready for action.

The three illustrations above show the sequence of action for taking a ball at mid-height. The sequence below shows taking a higher, wider rising ball at shoulder height.

The right foot moves across to bring the head into line with the ball. The hands give as they take the ball.

The weight transfers to the inside leg as the ball is carried to the stumps.

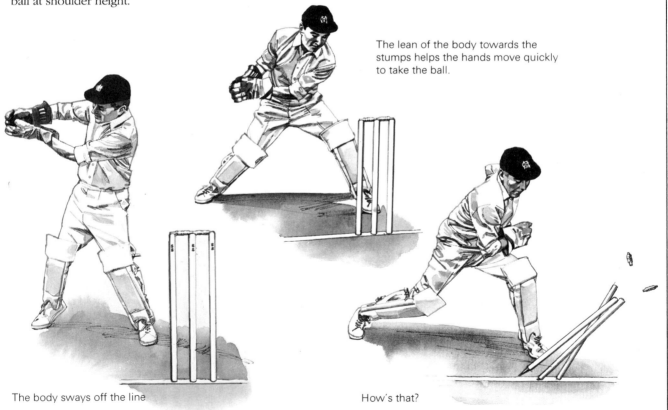

The lean of the body towards the stumps helps the hands move quickly to take the ball.

The body sways off the line

How's that?

'For behind the abrasive front was a thoughtful, astute and humorous man, whose players, when he led WA, were totally committed to him. The Australian Cricket Board, however, were not, but their prejudice was not based on technical consideration, such as having a wicketkeeper captain. For them he was tarred with the same brush as Ian Chappell, the brush of revolution and extremism. Greg Chappell with his dignified air they could stomach as captain, but they refused to swallow Marsh; this was a major mistake.'

Incidentally, Marsh does not agree with the argument that the wicketkeeper is too preoccupied to captain a side (there have been remarkably few wicketkeeper-captains). He believes that the keeper is in the best position to observe a batsman or a bowler and that this should be a tremendous advantage for a captain. Unfortunately, he was never given the opportunity by the Australian Cricket Board to prove this at international level.

EQUIPMENT

Rod Marsh has witnessed huge changes in the wicketkeeper's kit – 'my first pair of gloves had masses of leather hanging over the edges'. Since he reckons that it is easiest to catch a ball with bare hands, he is a strong advocate of having gloves of as small a size as possible. When Brian Close acted as emergency keeper for Somerset, he went one stage further and promptly disposed of the gloves, but I would stop short of recommending that for normal mortals.

Whereas Alan Knott liked at least two pairs of inner gloves, Marsh preferred just one, made of the thinnest chamois leather. I inspected his hands and they look unblemished. He worked on the well-worn theory that prevention is better than cure. Before a fielding session he would tape some foam rubber about the size of a 10p piece on the palm of his hand between his first and third finger. He would also tape up the first joint of his longest fingers, his little fingers and sometimes his thumbs; these were the areas he regarded as most vulnerable. His biggest mistake, he recalls, was having his hands X-rayed in England, only to discover a mass of floating bones: 'if you know about it, it hurts more'.

Curiously it was England's current keeper, Jack Richards, who introduced Marsh to cut down pads. Richards

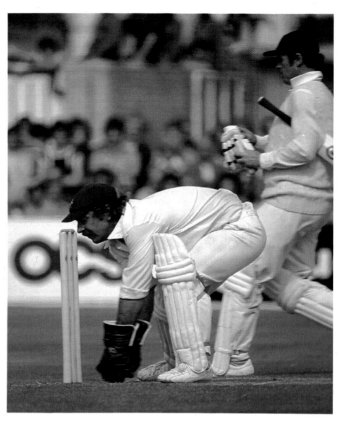

A fearless Rod Marsh ready for action. Notice his position behind the stumps and how close he is to them. Here he is seen wearing conventional pads. However, he was soon converted to 'cut down' pads when introduced to them by England keeper Jack Richards in 1977.

gave him a pair in England in 1977, which Marsh wore for a year before persuading an Australian company to make some of similar design. They offer sufficient protection, while allowing far greater mobility. A good keeper rarely gets hit on the pads.

Unlike Knott and Taylor, his two great English contemporaries, Marsh never wore a floppy hat, but always a cap. This was not because he reckoned that he looked more debonair in a cap – that has never been one of Marsh's prime considerations – but for a more practical reason. He explains, 'Mick Malone (Western Australia and Australia) was one of the best outfielder catchers I've seen and he always used to put up his hand in line with the ball to help judge its speed and trajectory. Baseball fielders do the same thing. I found that the peak of the cap acted as a viewfinder, giving me a better sight of the ball.'

Marsh never wore a short-sleeved shirt when keeping. A wicketkeeper must always be prepared to dive and it is easy to pick up grazes and scabs on the elbow, particularly on the harder grounds of the subcontinent. Long-sleeved shirts give a little more protection.

And he always wore a box.

PREPARATION

Alan Knott was sensitive about his health and fitness; he thought it essential to exercise constantly on the field and to be on the alert off it. He fell ill in Delhi one evening and, in the middle of the night, knocked on the physiotherapist's door, bearing a sample of what had recently been in his stomach for a diagnosis. Marsh would not have paid so much attention to detail and, as a few airline stewards can confirm, he didn't regard the odd beer as being detrimental to his game. Yet his fitness record is remarkable; he never missed a first class game through injury. Before each season he concentrated upon strengthening his legs by doing hundreds of squats and plenty of running over short distances, simulating a keeper's dash up to the wicket for a run out. At a practice session or before a match, Marsh, wearing his gloves, would ask someone to hit him a series of catches from a distance of 10 yards. Once he felt that he was gloving the ball well, he stopped; he didn't want to lose concentration and pick up bad habits. Then he might practise catching with bare hands on a slip cradle with one other person; these catches would not travel quickly but he would stand as close as possible to the cradle, thereby improving his reflexes. This exercise often developed into a 5-day Test with his partner, or even a 5 Test Series – Marsh enjoyed introducing a strong competitive element into his training. He did not like to practise in groups of three or four, but on his own; he much preferred intensive catching practice as it is more efficient and more demanding.

Remembering Viv Richards' observation that if he was catching well, he was batting well, I asked Marsh if the same applied to him. The answer was 'No'. In fact, if he had kept badly and felt that he had let the side down, the desire to compensate often meant that he batted better – so bang went another generalization.

STANDING BACK

Playing in Perth, and in the era of Lillee and Thomson, meant that Marsh more than most keepers spent a higher percentage of his time standing back. Of his 355 Test victims (a world record) only 12 were stumped; by comparison, 46 of Godfrey Evans' 219 victims in Test cricket were stumped.

Phil Edmonds bowls a bouncer to Richard Hadlee. Such a delivery will have startled not only the batsman but also the keeper; in this instance it is Bob Taylor. Nonetheless Taylor has taken the ball cleanly. I presume that Edmonds thought the seamers should be bowling. 1st Test, England v New Zealand, The Oval, July 1983.

When standing back to the likes of Thomson or Lillee, Marsh waited for the ball on the balls of his feet, his weight forward and his hands on the ground since 'it is easier for a keeper or slip fielder to come up rather than move down'. If a right handed bowler was bowling at a right handed batsman, he placed his left foot on or just outside the line of off stump. He aimed to take the ball at waist height as it was coming down. Playing in Perth in the Seventies with Lillee tearing in downwind meant that he could be at least 25 yards back. If a batsman pushed a quick single to cover (and I suspect quite a few were eager to scramble down to the other end), it was impossible for Marsh to get to the stumps in time; he would dutifully set off, sprinting flat out, quite often not stopping until he reached the non striker's end, yet he'd still be too late. Not surprisingly, he resented

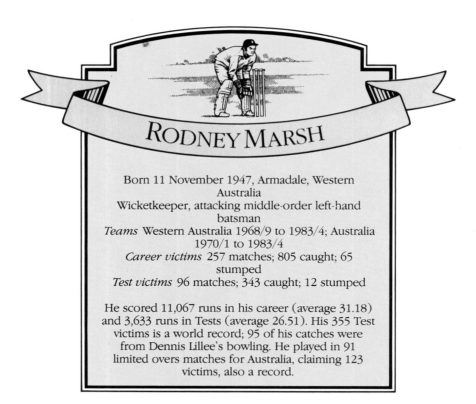

RODNEY MARSH

Born 11 November 1947, Armadale, Western
Australia
Wicketkeeper, attacking middle-order left-hand
batsman
Teams Western Australia 1968/9 to 1983/4; Australia
1970/1 to 1983/4
Career victims 257 matches; 805 caught; 65
stumped
Test victims 96 matches; 343 caught; 12 stumped

He scored 11,067 runs in his career (average 31.18)
and 3,633 runs in Tests (average 26.51). His 355 Test
victims is a world record; 95 of his catches were
from Dennis Lillee's bowling. He played in 91
limited overs matches for Australia, claiming 123
victims, also a record.

media criticism of his tardy arrival, since, as Marsh so
eloquently explained, 'Carl Lewis would have struggled'.

Before each match, Marsh inspected the wicket to assess
its likely pace and bounce and, combining this information
with his knowledge of his bowlers, he decided how deep
to stand. Towards the end of his career his initial judgement was rarely more than a foot out. If two hands could
be used, he used them, preferably catching the ball in his
right glove with the hands overlapping: yet he was so
confident when making diving catches down the leg side,
that in my innocence I'd assumed that he was left handed.

For Marsh, footwork was the key. He concentrated on
taking the ball on the inside of his body. If the ball was
outside off stump, he tried to move quickly to his right,
taking the ball on his left hand side; similarly, if the ball was
down the leg side he liked to take it on his right-hand side.
This obviously required greater movement, and therefore
greater effort, and this may be one reason why English
keepers rarely adopt this method; the sheer volume of
cricket in an English summer prevents such extravagances.
It also demands considerable mental discipline to move
that extra yard at 5.45 in the evening after a long day in the
field.

Yet the advantages are obvious. If the batsman snicks the
ball, the keeper is in a far better position to allow for the
deviation. Also, by covering more ground he is, in effect,
creating an extra fieldsman, something which all captains
dream about. In recent years, many players and a few
commentators noticed that the Australian slip cordon
covered more ground than its English counterpart; this
was mainly because of Rodney Marsh.

When practising, then, Marsh was most conscious of his
feet. 'If your feet are moving well, invariably you're gloving
well because your timing is right. Rhythm starts with your
feet; it's like a dance form if you get it right. As in batting, if
the feet are in the right position, so is the head,' he says. In
practice, he would often bounce the ball back to a
batsman, move to take the ball on the inside and then
move back to the starting point; he would keep repeating
this for about five minutes, creating a rhythm. The whole
process may not have impressed Lionel Blair but it did Rod
Marsh the world of good.

Even when the wicketkeeper is standing back it is still a
tremendous advantage to know what sort of ball will be
bowled. Marsh was able to spot slight differences in a
bowler's approach and action, which gave him more time
to move into the best position to take the ball. Take, as an
example, Bob Massie, whose swing bowling in the Lord's
Test of 1972 (he took 16–137) reached heights that he
would never surpass. He used to run up a few inches wider
for his inswinger and Marsh, unlike the English batsman in
1972, could detect those few inches and move accordingly.

Of course, he had a special relationship with Dennis
Lillee. Before every ball he bowled, Lillee used to glance at
Marsh at the end of his mark and sometimes Marsh would

*Rod Marsh is perfectly balanced
as he takes the ball and
attempts a run out on Derek
Randall.
The wicketkeeper (along with
the umpire) is in the best
position to assess the merits of*
*such contests between batsmen
and fielding side. Therefore,
part of his job is to appeal.
Marsh took this role seriously
and worked on the principle
that if he thought it was out, he
made a noise. Brisbane, 1982.*

'call for' a particular delivery. 'If I put my hand up by my right shoulder, it meant a bouncer on off stump; if my hand was up by my left shoulder, a bouncer on leg stump. He always bowled the ball exactly where I called it. It was unbelievable. If I tapped my feet I wanted a yorker. Unfortunately, that was the one ball that Dennis never mastered. If he had had Garner's yorker he would have taken over 500 Test wickets. The tailenders just kept playing at and missing his perfect outswingers.'

Occasionally these ploys worked – 'maybe two or three times out of a hundred'. In a memorable one-day game in Perth, Western Australia were bowled out for 78 and yet won by 17 runs. Marsh will never forget the match. 'When Greg Chappell came in [for Queensland] I signalled for a leg side bouncer. I started moving as soon as Lillee was in his delivery stride. Chappell hooked, got a lot of bat on it and I caught the ball way down the leg side. Chappell couldn't believe it, nor could the TV commentators, who kept praising Western Australia's keeper; in fact the praise really belonged to Dennis. It was a sensational feeling.'

STANDING UP

Standing up to the wicket has always been regarded as the test of a true keeper, as Marsh explains. 'If you had brilliant fielders like Viv Richards or Ian and Greg Chappell keeping wicket they would cope easily standing back, but if you put them up to the stumps their first reaction would probably be to make half a step backwards; a natural keeper doesn't make that movement.'

Marsh would love to have played a couple of seasons in England on uncovered wickets, for that represents the ultimate challenge. He admits, 'Only after playing in Pakistan in 1982 on turning wickets with uneven bounce did I start calling myself a good keeper. I was really proud of myself on that tour; of course the other blokes didn't say anything because they didn't notice.

Right *Alan Knott played 95 times for England, despite the Kerry Packer interlude which interrupted his Test career. As* *well as being a top quality wicketkeeper, he was an impish, innovative batsman who seemed to relish a crisis.*

TAKING ON THE LEG SIDE

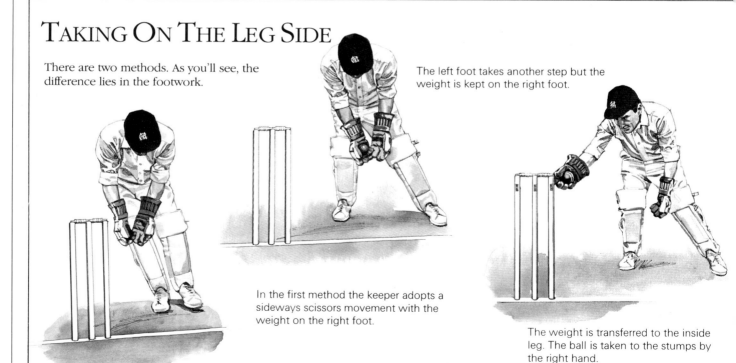

There are two methods. As you'll see, the difference lies in the footwork.

The left foot takes another step but the weight is kept on the right foot.

In the first method the keeper adopts a sideways scissors movement with the weight on the right foot.

The weight is transferred to the inside leg. The ball is taken to the stumps by the right hand.

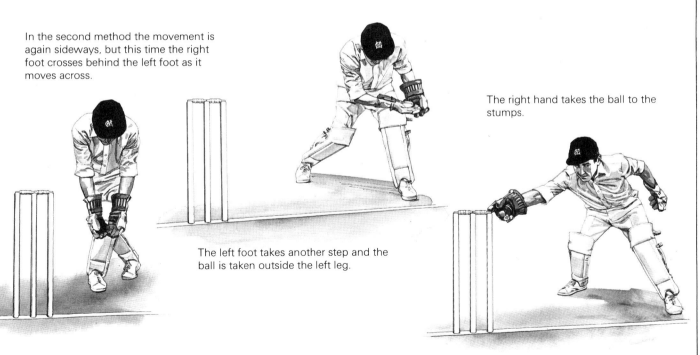

In the second method the movement is again sideways, but this time the right foot crosses behind the left foot as it moves across.

The right hand takes the ball to the stumps.

The left foot takes another step and the ball is taken outside the left leg.

'In 1971 Alan Knott told me that I must stay down until the ball pitches, so if someone bowls a full toss you don't come up at all. That's what I practise with guys throwing or bowling the ball to me. I never go in behind a batsman in the nets; it's far too dangerous.'

The keeper must assume that he is going to take every ball, even if he can't see it. 'You know where it was last, you know which way it was heading and you assume you're going to get it: you must forget that the batsman's there.'

Catches up at the wicket are very difficult to make, especially if the ball has taken a deflection. Marsh reckons that it is possible to legislate for a deflection, but only to a minute degree. 'For instance, if a leg spinner is bowling there is always a fair chance of an outside edge, so you can move the hands in that direction with the ball running across the face of the glove; if there is a deflection, then you are more likely to cling on to it.'

Probably the hardest catch to take is from a batsman attempting to cut; the ball might come from a bottom or top edge and, to make matters worse, the bat is flashing in front of the keeper's face. But none is easy. The snick from a front foot shot deviates more, so problems arise there. Maybe the ideal keeper's catch is from a backward

defensive shot; he has good sight of the ball and there's little space for the ball to deviate. Keeping your hands relaxed and hoping for the best may not sound very scientific advice, but that is what Marsh suggests.

After the ball has been taken, the keeper should automatically come back to the stumps so that he's always in a position to whip off the bails if there is the remotest chance of a stumping. Remember the laws – the ball must be taken behind the stumps and the line is yours. Spin bowlers tend to become a little grumpy when a batsman is stranded down the wicket and the keeper has snatched at the ball in front of the stumps before triumphantly demolishing them.

It is vital to be able to pick the different types of delivery of a slow bowler. When Marsh first started playing cricket at the highest level, Australia's leading slow bowler was the New South Wales 'mystery' spinner Johnnie Gleeson. With wonderful simplicity, he quickly learnt to read him: 'The first ball I received from Gleeson looked like an off spinner but turned out to be a leg spinner, so I decided that anything different to that must be going the other way. Then I studied his hands and I discovered that he placed them on the ball differently for his off spinner and leg spinner before he started his run up, so I knew what he was going to bowl. When playing against New South Wales I used to stand at the non striker's end and give a little signal to our batsmen and I was always right.'

The keeper (or the batsman) has three chances to pick the bowler: 1, by observing a change in his run up or action; 2, by watching his hand closely; and 3, by spotting which way the ball is spinning through the air. If all three methods prove unsuccessful, have a chat with the bowler and concoct a code system – but this is definitely a last resort. It is a trifle humiliating for a 'class' keeper and also you should ask yourself, 'Can I trust the bowler completely?'

RUN OUTS, LIMITED OVERS, CONCENTRATION

In Australia, wicketkeepers, full of unbridled zeal, tend to spring up to the stumps even when the ball has been patted back to the bowler. Marsh, ever the pragmatist, does not believe in rushing up to the stumps to no purpose, especially in temperatures of about 100°F (38°C). The keeper's prime job is to hold those snicks and there's no point in tiring yourself out and suffering a subsequent loss of concentration, just for show.

But you have to be prepared to take off after every ball; once the batsman has played his shot, the keeper's sight and hearing will determine whether or not he dashes to the wicket. Obviously, if there's any chance of a run out you must get to the stumps straight away. The golden rule is that the stumps must be between the keeper and the fielder. Ignore the batsman and whip the bails off as quickly as possible. Nearby fielders will usually tell the keeper to 'take 'em off' if the batsman is struggling.

In limited overs matches, however, the keeper should run up to the wicket every ball. Once there, he will often remove the glove from the throwing arm so that he can shy at the stumps at the bowler's end. When a bowler follows through and shies at the wickets the keeper doesn't have time to reach the stumps, so he then operates as a back-up fielder. Also, when the keeper is standing up, any ball within 5 yards of the stumps is his responsibility. An alert, fleet-footed keeper can prevent many of those frustrating quick singles.

Keeping in limited overs cricket is, according to Rod Marsh, 'hard work and it's lonely', and it can be more

Left *Dean Jones is stumped by Jack Richards. Stumpings are relatively easy when the ball goes past the outside edge of the bat, but when they pass between bat and pad the keeper has problems.*

Above *The wicketkeeper should always be on the alert for run-out chances. Here, Bob Taylor has sprinted up to the wicket in order to run out Sunil Gavaskar. 1st Test, England v India, Edgbaston, 1979.*

difficult to concentrate as a result. Marsh often relied upon having company to aid his concentration. 'Someone once told me that the human mind cannot concentrate for any more than 20 minutes at 100 per cent, so I reckoned it was important to break my concentration. As soon as the bowler turned at his mark, then I switched on. Once the ball was dead I switched off.' Then he would allow his mind to go anywhere, unless he was helping to plot the batsman's downfall. He would invariably chatter to the slips about anything – from the likely winner of the Melbourne Cup to whether he might permit himself a beer that evening. But when the bowler turned the chat had to stop, partly out of courtesy to the batsman, partly to recover his concentration.

THE KEEPER AS MOTIVATOR

One of the most important elements of a keeper's task has nothing to do with technique or glovework. I refer to the keeper's role as the fulcrum of the fielding side; he is the sergeant major, the motivator.

Marsh again: 'The keeper must set an example, since the

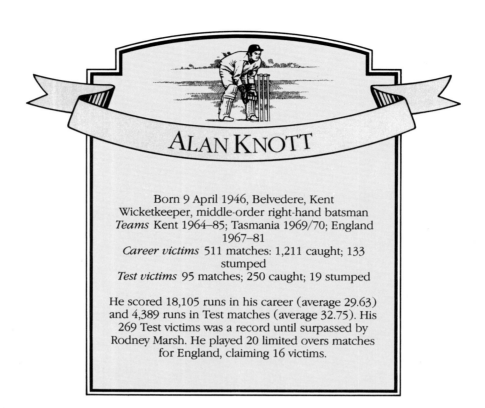

ALAN KNOTT

Born 9 April 1946, Belvedere, Kent
Wicketkeeper, middle-order right-hand batsman
Teams Kent 1964–85; Tasmania 1969/70; England
1967–81
Career victims 511 matches: 1,211 caught; 133
stumped
Test victims 95 matches; 250 caught; 19 stumped

He scored 18,105 runs in his career (average 29.63)
and 4,389 runs in Test matches (average 32.75). His
269 Test victims was a record until surpassed by
Rodney Marsh. He played 20 limited overs matches
for England, claiming 16 victims.

whole standard of the fielding drops if the keeper is being lazy. I made it very plain to my fielders that I set the standard and if any of them didn't reach it, then I let them know that I wasn't happy about it. By the same token, I gave plenty of praise when it was deserved.'

The captain often has too much on his mind to be constantly cajoling his men, yet it still surprised me to learn that Ian Chappell seldom criticized or shouted at his own players on the field, nor did he ever praise them. Marsh spent eight years desperately trying to get a 'well done' out of his skipper to no avail; yet Chappell's silence acted as a great motivating force for Marsh, who doggedly kept striving for that elusive compliment.

The keeper can also act as a great stimulus for the bowler. In my first one-day international I was grateful for the presence of David Bairstow bellowing all sorts of encouragement from behind the stumps, even if I found a large proportion of it incomprehensible. In *The Art of Captaincy*, Brearley acknowledges this role: 'The wicket-keeper is crucial. Bob Taylor would constantly and energetically encourage the English fast bowlers. He and I would often take turns in running to Willis at the end of an over, scuttling along beside his giant strides.'

As well as being a motivator, he must also be a foreman in these days of minimum over rates and penalties for failure to meet the required rate. The keeper should try to be first in position at the beginning of each over, while exhorting the rest to hurry up.

The keeper has the best viewing point on the ground and is therefore in an excellent position to help his captain with observations about the strengths and weaknesses of the batsman and the form of the bowler. In limited over games, Marsh had an important role for Australia in the setting of the field. The boundary fielders would always look to Marsh to see whether they were at the right angle relative to the close fielders. The captain might be at deep mid-off and unable to give assistance, so Marsh would often act as a fielding captain.

The keeper is also required to appeal. It may surprise a few Englishmen to learn that Marsh was often criticized by his team-mates for not appealing enough. His philosophy was straightforward and well worth emulating. If he thought that the batsman was out, he appealed very loudly; he was not in the habit of appealing for imaginary snicks. The cynics among you may regard this as bravado from a retired cricketer eager to make friends. Let me refer them to the Centenary Test in Melbourne in 1977. Derek Randall was already on his way back to the pavilion, having seen Marsh dive, roll over and emerge with the ball. However, Marsh indicated that the ball hadn't carried and Randall was recalled. Brearley, who played in that game, notes in *The Art of Captaincy* that 'in the context of the match – we were, at that time, well placed for a remarkable win and the Australians must have been tired and dispirited – Marsh's was a generous act.' But no more than I expect from readers of this book.

Alan Knott was a valued adviser to several England captain's, from Ray Illingworth to Mike Brearley. The keeper has an excellent vantage point from which to assess the game.

In limited overs cricket he is the player best placed to check the angles of the fielders. Here Knott seems to be making an adjustment to the field for his captain.

THE
LEADER

'A team functions best when the captain takes a high profile and calls the shots.'

JOHN INVERARITY

Mike Gatting leads out the team at Old Trafford; 1st Test, England v Pakistan, 1987.

To be captain is the most rewarding role in cricket; it is also the most demanding and the most treacherous. It is no wonder that the casualty rate among County captains is so high – in the early Seventies, for example, Derbyshire had four captains in five years and in the Fifties Somerset managed three in just one season. The captain inevitably becomes the scapegoat in defeat, but on the other hand he's not necessarily regarded as being the architect of victory. In May 1985, David Gower, having become just the third English Test captain ever to return victorious from a tour of India, was greeted at his breakfast table by the headlines 'Gower Must Go' after two one-day defeats at the hands of the Australians. Within four months the Ashes had been regained, Gower having scored 732 runs in the series, and he seemed as secure as a Tory in Tunbridge Wells. After another six months and a tour to the West Indies he was unceremoniously dumped, no doubt more than a little confused.

At every level the captain's job is never done. On an international tour he has the ultimate responsibility for all cricketing decisions, with the manager, assistant manager and vice-captain acting as his props; he must be a diplomat, a press officer, a strategist, a confidant and a disciplinarian. He sets the tone for the entire touring party. At County level, he often has to arrange for X to take a detour to Malmesbury to pick up Y who has been playing in the second team, while explaining to disgruntled Z why he's been dropped. Further down the line, at club and village level, it's generally his 'phone that rings on Saturday morning when his opening bowler's eldest has developed chicken pox while the wife is visiting the in-laws. In addition to all that, he must assume total command on the field as well as justify his position in the team with runs or wickets. Yet there's no better and more triumphant sensation in cricket than leading your side to victory – and the more unlikely the victory, the greater the exhilaration. It is said that Richie Benaud, after England had been defeated in the Old Trafford Test of 1961 thanks to his final, desperate ploy of bowling leg spinners around the wicket, just sat down in the dressing room with a beer and burst out laughing – a supremely happy man.

There's no simple identikit for the good captain. For Yorkshire, Somerset and England Brian Close was an instinctive, occasionally irrational leader prepared to pursue any hunch, however ridiculous it seemed to his colleagues, while his contemporary Ray Illingworth (Leice- stershire and England) was ruthlessly logical and methodical. Both, however, were successful. Tony Greig and Tony Lock were rarely regarded as shrewd tacticians, but both were able to instil into their sides some of their own zest and enthusiasm for the challenge. In contrast, the two most successful captains I have played under, Brian Rose at Somerset and Graeme Wood in Western Australia, appeared to be most unlikely leaders before their appointments. Both were shy, insular characters, yet they soon surprised everyone with their drive and ability to communicate with their players, however quietly. The most striking common denominator among all these captains is simply that they remained true to their own character. Geoff Miller, an easy-going, affable all rounder, once told me how he tried to change himself into a rigid disciplinarian when he first became captain of Derbyshire, but soon recognized that it didn't work. Cricket teams spend too many hours together to enable anyone to maintain a convincing façade.

At this point I'll direct those of you who wish to read a detailed analysis of the captain's role to Mike Brearley's book *The Art of Captaincy*. Brearley's Test record as captain is phenomenal, even taking into account the Packer intrusion and the fact that he never led England against the West Indies in a Test series; out of 31 Tests he won 18 and lost just 4. *The Art of Captaincy* is equally impressive. Maybe I should have interviewed him, but since he has expressed his views so succinctly in print it seemed a rather futile exercise to get him to reiterate them. Instead, I spoke to John Inverarity, who is regarded in Australia with almost the same reverence as Brearley in England. Admittedly Inverarity never captained Australia (in retrospect, it is bewildering that the Australian Board preferred Graham Yallop in 1978), but he led Western Australia to four Sheffield Shields in the space of six seasons in the Seventies.

Apart from the length of their international careers, Brearley and Inverarity have much else in common with each other; they are both academics, captaining their respective university sides at the age of 20 and using their respective intellects to great advantage on a cricket field (this isn't always the case with intelligent players). Both of them were prolific run-scorers outside the Test arena (Inverarity has scored more Sheffield Shield runs than anyone), yet both faltered at Test level; and they were both excellent captains.

Below *Gower and England's current captain and vice-captain, respectively Mike Gatting and John Emburey, must have been influenced by Mike Brearley. With the odd exception, Brearley had the knack of getting the best out of his players. He was also extremely adept at handling the press, an increasingly important role for international captains. Like Benaud before him, rather than feel threatened by them, Brearley used the press to his own advantage.*

Right *David Gower holding the most coveted trophy in cricket – the Ashes. Under his phlegmatic, low-key leadership England regained the Ashes in 1985; yet within six months he was deposed. Gower has sometimes been criticized for being 'too laid back', yet a captain cannot desert his own personality on appointment. Gower the stern disciplinarian would have been totally unconvincing.*

ROBERT JOHN INVERARITY

Born 31 January 1944, Perth, Western Australia
Opening right-hand batsman, slow left-arm bowler,
good slip field
Teams Western Australia 1962/3 to 1978/9; South
Australia 1979/80 to 1984/5; Australia 1968–72
Career batting 223 matches; 11,777 runs; highest
score 187; average 35.90
Career bowling 223 matches; 221 wickets; best
bowling 7–86; average 30.67
Test batting 6 matches; 174 runs; highest score 56;
average 17.40
Test bowling 6 matches; 4 wickets; best bowling
3–26; average 23.25
Catches Career 251; Test 4

An outstanding captain, he led Western Australia for
six seasons in the 1970s and won the Sheffield
Shield in four of them.

SELECTING THE CAPTAIN

England and Australia have traditionally adopted different approaches regarding selection of their captain, which partly explains the disparity in Test appearances between Brearley and Inverarity. England have always selected the captain first, therefore placing greater emphasis on 'leadership qualities', and then eleven other players are added. In Australia, the twelve best players are chosen and from this number they select the most suitable captain.

I asked Inverarity which method he advocated.

'A selector's prime responsibility, whether it be at international, State, club or school level, is to select the team that will perform best. I realize that this is a very straightforward statement, but it is complex in the process of its execution. I have no doubt that when Brearley was captain of England he was the greatest single contributor to that team, even though he was far from being the best player; and the major part of his contribution was through his captaincy. I thought Brearley was a superb captain both in terms of strategy and in the way he enhanced the games of the

other ten players in the side. England were simply a much better side when he was there. (This was vividly demonstrated in the 1981 Ashes series in England.) If someone is available who would improve the performance of the team, despite being no more than an average player, then I think there's no question that he should be included. However, if there is no one person obviously superior to all the others as captain you can't go far wrong picking the eleven best players and choosing a captain from among them. I don't like saying you should use the Australian method or the English method; it just depends on who's available. The aim of the selectors, quite simply, should always be to select the unit which will perform best, and the captaincy influence is a major factor in team performance.'

John Inverarity batting against Worcestershire in 1972. This thoughtful, articulate schoolmaster captained Western Australia when Lillee and Marsh were reaching their prime, and he quickly gained their respect. Lillee and Marsh played with as much commitment for Western Australia as they did when wearing the baggy green caps of Australia.

Whichever system is used it is universally agreed that the captain need by no means be the best player in the team, though it is desirable that his place should not be in question. There is less general agreement as to whether, in an ideal world, the captain should be a batsman, bowler or wicketkeeper. Don Bradman, a batsman, argued that he should be a batsman. Ray Illingworth, an all rounder, maintained that he should be an all rounder and we've already heard that Rod Marsh reckoned that the wicketkeeper had the best possible vantage point for the job. I'm not sure that there is a 'right' answer but, historically, most captains have in fact been batsmen.

TEAM SELECTION

Again, there is a fundamental difference in approach between England and Australia. In England, at international and County level, the captain is automatically on the selection committee. Indeed in County cricket, since the captain is often the only member of the committee who has observed the performances of his players without interruption, he is usually the most influential. Brearley favours this method and I suspect that any County captain who was not a selector would be aghast and would probably refuse to continue.

At State and Test level in Australia, however, the captain is not on the selection committee and therefore has no formal influence on the choice of players. This is the system that Inverarity prefers.

'Ideally, there is a good relationship between the selectors and the captain and there are good lines of communication. The selectors consult the captain, who has the confidence to make suggestions but in the end leaves it entirely to the selectors to make the decision. In my experience, it is difficult for a captain or a coach to be a selector. A major part of the role of captain is to be a confidant to his players and he is less likely to achieve this effectively if the players know that

Jack Richards represented a successful gamble by the selectors for the Australian tour in 1986/7. Since they were concerned to solve the problem of England's early fragility, the selectors opted for Richards rather than French, who was regarded as the better keeper. Richards repaid their faith by keeping in excellent style and scoring a century at Perth.

he wields the axe. A good captain, while being rational and objective, is also inclined to be biased towards his players and less likely to support changes. I was never a selector and there was not a time when I was given players whom I didn't want.' [I suspect that Inverarity was quite forceful in his informal discussions with the selectors.] *'Certainly there were times when a player was left out whom I would have marginally preferred in the team, but I always found myself able to fully support the preferred player and the selectors' judgement. Most times discussion only occurs about one or two places with the great majority being automatic selections.'*

That is the Australian way of doing things, which I'm sure would gain little support in England. Indeed Bradman, in *The Art Of Cricket*, writes 'I am very much in favour in principle of the captain being a member of the selection committee'.

Enough of how the side is picked; the next problem is whom to pick.

Western Australia's success in the Seventies owed a great deal to its pace attack. This was not a deliberate policy on the part of Inverarity and his selectors, however; selection again depended on the players who were available at the time.

'I'd prefer a truly balanced attack with two quicks, a medium pace all rounder, a wrist spinner and a finger spinner. However, Western Australia often played a side stacked with fast/swing bowlers. This wasn't because I believed in them any more than spin bowlers; we simply picked our best bowlers and they happened to be fast or medium pacers. Also, the Western Australia Cricket Association wicket, as well as the club pitches in Perth, favoured this type of bowler. So our five bowlers might be McKenzie, Lillee and Massie, supported by two medium pace all rounders, Graeme Watson and Ian Brayshaw; often we would include leg spinner Tony Mann, but he might not bowl very much. In 1986/7 the English attack in Australia was well balanced and, I imagine, a good unit to captain (Dilley, DeFreitas or Small, Botham, Emburey and Edmonds). Australia tried to emulate this balance, but as the raw material wasn't there my sympathy was with the selectors.'

When selecting batsmen Inverarity, along with most captains, would ideally like a potent mixture of experienced grafters, uninhibited stroke players, and left and right handers, though it is almost impossible to achieve every desirable element when there may be just five batting spots available. Certainly he prefers one opener to be a 'dasher', who can launch the innings early, rather than have two dour, solid players.

Also, don't forget the selection of a wicketkeeper. Obviously it helps if he can bat. On England's 1986/7 tour to Australia Bruce French, arguably the best keeper in England, was replaced by Jack Richards, who is a better batsman. This decision was vindicated by a sparkling century by Richards in the Second Test, and the unfortunate French was reduced to the role of drinks waiter for the rest of the tour. The selection of the keeper should also be governed by the nature of your bowling attack. India, who rely mainly on spin, must have a keeper who excels up at the stumps; this is not so crucial for the West Indies.

TEAM PREPARATION

In Australia, a State side spends far more time and energy preparing for a season or a match than does an English County side. Western Australia's State squad begin weekly training sessions in June, even though the season doesn't start until October, and before each match there are two or three vigorous net sessions. In England, by contrast, each County side gathers in April, two or three weeks before the first match, and by the end of May net practices occur only sporadically. This is not because English County sides are particularly idle or slapdash; the difference stems from the disparity in the amount of cricket played. In England, a professional cricketer plays at least 110 days in a season, while a State player in Australia plays a maximum of 45. Let me give an example from my own experience. In England in 1986 I batted 36 times for Somerset in first class cricket, while in Australia in 1986/7 just 10 times for Western Australia (admittedly I was rarely called upon in the second innings). Not only is there more time for an Australian to prepare, therefore, but also each day's cricket assumes far greater importance for him.

With opportunities so limited it's hardly surprising that Australians take more precautions before a game to ensure that everything is in prime working order. Inverarity was meticulous in his planning and preparation during the Australian winter. He often spent three nights a week with small groups from the State squad; for example, one night might be devoted to improving the batting prowess of his bowlers, another to the wicketkeepers. This strikes an Englishman as being remarkably selfless and beyond the call of duty, but Inverarity admits that these sessions were in part generated by his own ego: 'The success of the team meant a lot to me as an individual; if everybody could contribute a little bit extra, then the team would benefit. For the same reason, if Richie Benaud was in Perth I tried to make sure that he met up with our leg spinner Tony Mann; I was keen to get Benaud to talk to Mann because this would probably make Mann a better bowler and us a better cricket team.'

It is invariably true that the more effort a team expends in preparation the more determined it is not to waste all that effort when the matches start. This may be one way in which it is possible to create that nebulous though vital element – team spirit, which was, and still is, regarded as a characteristic of Western Australia sides. Inverarity says:

'We used to talk at length about fostering team spirit. We said that we could only honestly call ourselves a team if we could genuinely enjoy the success of other members of the team as much as our own. I was fortunate that there were a lot of players of similar age, who got on extraordinarily well. Also, in Perth at that time, there was a strong adolescent type of feeling in the community of "us against the rest". We were the outcasts in the West, who had often been patronized and given short shrift by the Eastern states. I was more than happy to exploit this feeling, which was a tremendous way to build harmony and close ranks against the rest.

'I remember my first Eastern states tour vividly. In Sydney, on a flat wicket, we scored 424; New South Wales declared at 425 for 1; in the second innings we scored 269 and Benaud, their captain, decided to send in their Nos. 4 and 5 to open the batting and gain some practice; they won the match by nine wickets, so

When Botham's spell as England captain ended, he was adamant that Brearley was the man to replace him. Botham had enjoyed most of his international success under Brearley, so his preference was hardly surprising. Despite their obvious differences, these two formed a close relationship.

in the whole game we had dismissed just two players. In Brisbane, Queensland scored 600 and the same happened in Melbourne. We were the chopping blocks. Our captain, Barry Shepherd, kept saying, "Soak every bit of this up, son; our day will come." The Eastern states were very good and very condescending. When I became captain, with Ian Brayshaw as my deputy, at most team meetings we'd remind the players of our experiences. That, coupled with Western Australia's isolation, helped to foster unity within the team.'

To a lesser extent, this atmosphere prevailed in the Somerset side of the late Seventies, with Brian Rose and Peter Denning providing us with the gory details of the past to spur us on.

THE ROLE OF COACH/MANAGER

Most first class captains are now supported by a coach and over the last 15 years several sides in County cricket have also had a team manager, although arguments still continue as to what his responsibilities should be or indeed whether the position is worthwhile. There is plenty of contradictory evidence. Middlesex and Essex, England's two most successful counties in the last decade, have prospered without the assistance of a manager. Ray Illingworth, when he returned to Yorkshire as manager, was unable to enhance the team's performances and yet when he decided to come out of retirement and captain the side results clearly improved. Norman Gifford at Warwickshire, however, has been very grateful for the presence of manager David Brown: 'I've found that David eases my burden by dealing with net practices, training, travelling and rooming arrangements, and it is helpful to bounce ideas off him while a game is in progress.' When Inverarity was captain of Western Australia he felt that there were certain responsibilities that he wished to share and he was instrumental in having Daryl Foster assigned to the team as coach.

'I was keen to develop the role of coach/manager who, under the direction of the captain, could run practices and take much of the responsibility for players' fitness and pre-match warm-ups. The first morning of a match is a hectic time for a captain. I wanted to have a

good net, since I was usually batting at No. 3, and some catches; I needed to assess the nature of the wicket, help decide upon the twelfth man and carry out the toss. It was a great help having someone supervising warm-ups and practice who didn't have to attend to his own game. Also, there was a period in Australia soon after the advent of World Series cricket when a lot of inexperienced cricketers were thrust into the captaincy and many of them needed propping up by a coach or a manager. Ten years later, however, it concerns me a little that captains look too much for a prop; in my view a team functions best when the captain takes a high profile and calls the shots.'

So Inverarity welcomed assistance, but there was no doubt that he was the man in charge of the team and in my experience this is the only way a cricket team can function effectively. Where there is a manager, his role needs to be clearly defined and it must not undermine in any way the authority of the captain. In *The Art of Captaincy* Brearley observes that 'the county side with a good captain has no urgent need for a manager; while no manager, however brilliant, can make up for a bad captain'.

THE TOSS

Casual observers of a cricket match must be amazed by the attention given to the pitch on the morning of a game. Often a procession of players can be seen walking out to the middle, where they poke and prod the unsuspecting wicket; they bang it with their bats, they force knives into it and they even get down on their knees to caress the blades of grass with the palms of their hands. Most players learn to keep their opinions of the pitch to themselves so that later in the day they can castigate the captain about his decision to bat or bowl without compromising themselves. The captain, however, must commit himself before the match begins, and this decision often causes him considerable torment.

One such occasion was the Adelaide Test of 1982/3. Bob Willis, England's captain, favoured batting first but his lieutenants Gower and Botham, mindful of England's early order fragility against Thomson, Lawson and Hogg, finally persuaded him to field. Within half an hour it became clear that this decision had been a mistake, as the ball refused to

Ian Botham and Greg Chappell toss up before the Centenary Test at Lord's, 1980. By this time – about half an hour before the start of the game – the captain has decided who should be twelfth man and whether he wants to bat or bowl first. These seemingly straightforward decisions can cause much agonizing.

deviate in any direction. Willis later deeply regretted that he had been swayed against his better judgement and for a while this decision severely affected his confidence as captain. In that Test, Australia scored 438 in their first innings and won by eight wickets after enforcing the follow on. It is this sort of experience that makes captains wary of putting the opposition in first.

Tony Lock, Inverarity's predecessor in Western Australia, reckoned that nine times out of ten you bat first without thinking; the tenth time you think seriously about fielding but still bat. Inverarity declined to adopt such an inflexible approach. He often inserted the opposition and his reasoning was straightforward. 'The Western Australia Cricket Association wicket was a good batting pitch on the first day, but it was even better on the second and probably at its best on the fourth. My trump cards were McKenzie, Lillee and Massie; the sooner we played them in the game the better, and they preferred bowling when there was a little moisture left in the pitch.' Indeed, it's often a sign of a confident side if they want to take the option to bowl first, provided the motivation comes from an eagerness to dismiss the opposition rather than a reluctance to 'face the music'.

The captain must try to predict how a wicket will play; he's more likely to be able to do this on his home ground, often after consultation with the groundsman. A trend has developed in County cricket whereby the captain might

'order' a wicket to suit his requirements. When Nottinghamshire won the County Championship in 1981 the groundsman at Trent Bridge produced a series of green, seaming wickets that suited their ace Richard Hadlee down to the ground. It is dangerous to be too dogmatic about a pitch's likely behaviour, but here are a few broad guidelines.

If the wicket is hard and well grassed, the ball is likely to bounce and seam, suiting the faster bowlers; this type of wicket would certainly tempt a captain to field first on winning the toss.

Sometimes the pitch, though not well grassed, has retained a lot of moisture, in which case the ball is likely to grip and deviate for both seamers and spinners; again, there would be a temptation to field before it dries out.

If the pitch is dry and therefore likely to crumble (the Sydney Cricket Ground has provided a good example of this in recent years), a captain would unhesitatingly bat first, using the surface at its most accommodating to batsmen in the hope that his spinners might dominate on the second and third days when the ball is more likely to grip as the soil becomes looser.

On what is reckoned to be a good batting surface most captains would elect to bat first and compile a large total, thereby putting pressure on the opposition even if the wicket doesn't deteriorate. If the pitch doesn't quite satisfy any of these criteria the best thing to do is to lose the toss.

TEAM TALKS

Before taking the field, most captains feel obliged to say something. In 1978, when Somerset were chasing their first-ever trophy, our captain, Brian Rose, informed us that 'this was the most important game in the club's history' for five games in a row. Another Somerset captain, before a vital one-day game at Swansea, confined himself to 'Get stuck in, back up and watch the sandy bits' and, of course, we won. In England, with so much cricket, it would be ridiculous for a captain to deliver a heartrending call to arms five days a week, but for a Test match or a State game in Australia there may be more expansive discussion.

When Bob Willis was captain of England, for instance, the strengths and weaknesses of every opposition batsman would be analyzed in some detail and our batsmen would also discuss the opposition bowlers. Occasionally such discussion can become too elaborate and end up confusing the bowlers rather than helping them, since the best place to bowl at 95 per cent of batsmen is on a good length at off stump. I remember Willis, before a one-day international in New Zealand, writing down on an envelope the exact fielding position of every player when I came on to bowl my off spinners. Quite sensibly, we wanted to ensure

Ray Illingworth leads out Yorkshire at Edgbaston in 1982. Leading a County side is precarious and demanding. Originally, Illingworth had been appointed manager but found himself frustrated. When he took over the captaincy results improved. His example emphasizes the point that the captain, not the manager, has the most important position in a club.

that the best fielders were in the most important positions. I carried the envelope out on to the field and everything went superbly, with fielders moving into position with military precision, until a left hander took strike and Derek Randall was left wandering around like a headless chicken. It was a good idea, though.

Unusually, Graeme Wood, captain of Western Australia since 1985, prefers coach Daryl Foster to lead team meetings. It is a task Foster takes very seriously. For several days before the match he mulls over the points he wants to stress; at the meeting itself he attempts to involve the players and to prompt them into making the relevant points. Foster admits, 'We all fall into the habit of preaching occasionally and labouring a point, but since I haven't been a first class player it would be stupid to pontificate as if I had.' Foster believes that his training as a teacher of physical education has helped him to fulfil this role more effectively.

Inverarity pinpoints the two goals of a team meeting – motivation and the imparting of information. These two elements are linked. 'By analyzing an opponent, a team can develop a strategy of how best to oppose him. This analysis includes anticipating the way a player is likely to think and approach his game, and how he might be frustrated. A further advantage to these discussions is that the whole team shares something, and out in the middle this can heighten interest and be a linking medium which aids concentration.' Two examples: Geoff Boycott was extremely adept at pushing the ball wide of mid-on for a single; if the mid-on and mid-wicket were made aware of this, they were more likely to be alert when he took strike. John Wright of Derbyshire and New Zealand is an excellent player but a fallible judge of a run and this piece of valuable information should ensure that the infield are actively looking for runs outs when Wright is batting.

Before the game, the captain should also discuss with his bowlers the desired field placements with adjustments for particular players. For instance, a County side playing at Worcester would be foolish not to adjust their field when Graeme Hick and Phil Neale are batting together. Hick hits a full length ball on off stump back past the bowler, while Neale would hit it between cover point and extra cover.

Undoubtedly it helps if the team is aware of some sort of overall strategy before taking the field, but it is equally important to recognize that even the best laid plans can go awry once you are out there. This is when the captain's wit and ingenuity are most tested.

Brearley takes his time positioning the field during the memorable Headingley Test against Australia in 1981. Attention to detail is crucial in a closely contested finish.

IN THE FIELD

Inverarity explains the psychology of fielding thus:

'When a batsman goes to the wicket he can experience something between two extremes. He may take guard, look around and feel at home. Nothing seems to be opposing him: cover point is not threatening and he's too deep; bat pad is chatting to the wicketkeeper. Everything is cosy and the batsman feels welcome. Alternatively, a fielding side can communicate combativeness and a lack of welcome, not through "sledging", which I deplore, but through their body language. The fielders are ready and they walk in aggressively and forbiddingly. I think that a cricket team should try to cultivate this atmosphere. A common saying in Australian Rules Football is that "you've got to want the ball". The same applies in cricket; second slip should be willing a catch to come; the cover fieldsman eager for a run-out chance. If you have eleven players in that frame of mind, focusing on the batsman, I'm sure he feels that hostility. Andrew Hilditch once said to me – and it was music to my ears – that when he went out to bat for New South Wales against Western Australia he felt that "I was not welcome; my presence was not to be tolerated and they just wanted to get rid of me; they knew my weaknesses and they were hell bent on exploiting them".'

So much for motivation, but even if all eleven of them are in a really positive frame of mind, the fielding side will struggle if they're all standing in the wrong place. The good captain ensures that his fielders constantly have an eye on him so that they can be moved without recourse to frantic arm waving and throaty yells. It helps if the captain has a regular fielding position – first slip provides an excellent vantage point if he can catch, mid-off if he can't – since then he can be easily located.

The captain has nine fielders at his disposal and ultimately it is his decision how many should be used to attack, and how many to defend. (For a diagram showing the fielding positions available to the captain, see p. 107.) However, the field setting should be done in close conjunction with the bowler. Inverarity encouraged his bowlers to know what field placements they preferred and often they would echo the discussions that he had instigated before the game. Bowlers bowl better if they are happy with their field and the ideal situation for Inverarity was that the bowler suggested exactly what he wanted him to suggest. Sometimes negotiation and compromise are required and we've already noted how Brearley and Edmonds occasionally failed to agree upon what was the best option. Inverarity recalls that there were times when Dennis Lillee wanted something outrageous: 'Often I'd let him have his own way because when his tail was up and he was trying to prove a point, he was unstoppable.' He cites another example, concerning the swing bowler Bob Massie.

'Paradoxically, it was more attacking if Massie bowled with three slips and a gully and two saving the single on the off side, rather than four slips and just one cover fieldsman. If he had a mid-off he usually bowled beautifully, but if you took mid-off away, he bowled three feet shorter and wouldn't swing the ball as menacingly because he felt naked and unprotected. He was a much better and more penetrating bowler with two run-savers and one less in the slips. Even if you said "I don't mind if you get hit through mid-off", he was far more effective when he was confident of having sufficient protection.'

The same principle can apply to finger spinners. On the surface, it seems far more attacking to have four men rather than two around the bat, but the bowler might then bowl flatter to protect himself. If the field is more defensive he may be prepared to attack more through variations of spin and flight, so the captain should be sensitive to the disposition of his bowler as well as the strengths and weaknesses of the batsman. Ideally he has a 'photostat' brain like Illingworth's, which logs a batsman's likes and dislikes in its filing cabinet, since different players feel pressure in different ways. Inverarity says: 'When I went out to bat against a spinner I always preferred the opposition captain to station extra short legs. I didn't feel threatened by them. I was more likely to feel ill at ease if these fielders were put in run-saving positions and I had difficulty in scoring and getting my innings moving. A captain needs to

Allan Border leads primarily by example. By his own admission he's not the best communicator in the world. However, here he seems to be making his point quite forcibly to wicketkeeper Tim Zoehrer. 5th Test, Australia v England, 1987.

JOHN MICHAEL BREARLEY OBE

Born 28 April 1942, Harrow, Middlesex
Opening right-hand batsman
Teams Cambridge Univ 1961–64; Middlesex
1961–83; England 1976–81
Career batting 455 matches; 25,185 runs; highest
score 312 not out; average 37.81
Test batting 39 matches; 1,442 runs; highest score
91; average 22.88
Catches Career 418; Test 52

He was an outstanding captain, leading Middlesex
from 1971 to 1982, during which time the County
Championship was won four times and the Gillette
Cup twice. He led England in 31 Test matches, and
was captain on four tours. Having defeated Australia
in home and away series, he was recalled to the Test
team and captaincy during the 1981 season, when
Botham was deposed, and led England to another
Ashes victory. He played in 25 limited overs matches
for England, scoring 510 runs (highest 78), average
24.28, with 12 catches.

read each opponent's frame of mind and manoeuvre his resources to gain a psychological advantage.'

The captain must also decide when to change the bowling. The West Indian Test side has recently removed much of the subtlety of this art; with their four-pronged pace attack a straightforward rotation or shift system is employed. Each bowler bowls for an hour (about six or seven overs) three times a day; occasionally the pattern is broken with a spell of off spin from Harper or Richards. Fortunately, most other sides have a more balanced, if less effective, attack which allows greater scope for an imaginative captain.

The pattern for most teams is to allow the fast/swing bowlers use of the ball while it is still shiny and hard; if they are not looking threatening then it is advisable to try all the available bowlers to see which type will be most effective on that particular surface. Of course it is in the interests of some sides not to adhere to this pattern. In the Sixties and Seventies, when India were playing at home, they would toss the ball to Gavaskar, hardly the most terrifying opening bowler in Test history, for a couple of overs so that he could remove the shine, thereby allowing their formidable spin trio of Bedi, Prasanna and Chandrasekhar

to set to work. While this might prove effective in Delhi, it may not necessarily be so at Derby.

Deciding when to remove a bowler from the attack requires tactical awareness and a certain amount of intuition. Obviously, if a bowler is bowling poorly, it is sensible to take him off; ideally this should be done before he has conceded several boundaries. Considerable captaincy skill is necessary to read the game and know one's own bowlers sufficiently well to consistently pull out the bowler the over before he indicates that he needs to be withdrawn from the attack. Much is often conceded by a bowler going one over too long and conclusively showing that a change is required. Sometimes a bowler may deliver a succession of half volleys that are smashed straight to the fielders and he will end up with rather a fortuitous maiden; this would be a good time to rest him since his confidence may remain intact. Conversely, if a bowler has been hit for three boundaries in one over it is sometimes worth

Although a prolific run-scorer in County cricket, Brearley rarely blossomed in the Test arena despite the feeling of security that his helmet gave him.

Few people argued about his worth to the side. On one tour he suggested dropping himself, but his co-selectors quickly rejected the idea.

gambling by letting him bowl another one, so that when he is recalled later in the day he is not so anxious about where the ball will land.

Alternatively, a bowler may be bowling perfectly well but without troubling the batsman, in which case it is best to try someone else. Often the mere act of changing the bowling can upset a batsman's rhythm and concentration; in addition he has to adjust to a different action and possibly a different type of swing or spin.

The captain should also be aware of the ideal length of spell for each of his bowlers. For instance, Keith Fletcher and Graham Gooch at Essex often use John Lever in long opening spells of ten or twelve overs; they know that this is what Lever prefers and they are confident that if his rhythm is awry in the first few overs, he is likely to rediscover it as he goes along. In contrast, Rodney Hogg of Australia was only effective if used in short bursts of about four or five overs; thereafter he would lose much of his pace and bite.

Each side should ideally contain both types – the shock bowler who gives everything for five overs in an attempt to blast the batsmen out, and the stock bowler who can bowl for long periods and test the batsman's patience and concentration.

When a side has one truly outstanding bowler such as Marshall at Hampshire, Hadlee at Nottinghamshire or Lillee for Western Australia it is obviously tempting to bowl him all the time, but it would be very foolish. These bowlers would never survive the season, especially in County cricket, unless handled sympathetically. For example, if Mark Nicholas, the Hampshire captain, has set his opponents a run chase he generally adopts the following policy. Marshall may only bowl three or four overs in his opening spell; then Nicholas will bowl his 'lesser' bowlers in the hope that they will pick up wickets while the batsmen are taking risks to attain their target. Crucially, he always has Marshall up his sleeve for one of two eventualities. Either Nicholas will recall him when the opposition is six or seven wickets down to deliver the coup de grace or when Marshall is needed to thwart the run chase. This ensures that chasing runs against Hampshire is a formidable proposition.

In the same way, Inverarity used Lillee carefully, though later in his career Lillee became an accomplished stock bowler if the conditions demanded. 'I was always aware of keeping enough of him back so that he would be able to charge in at a new batsman, since he was our most lethal strike bowler. If the score was 120–1, I'd often keep him in the wings and patiently try other avenues to get a breakthrough. When it came, it was good to be able to swing him into the attack on a fresh batsman.'

It is great to have a world class bowler in your side, but in recent years Essex have proved that it is not essential (with apologies to Lever, Foster and co). Certainly they have had a well-balanced attack of experienced bowlers, but no-one in the Marshall/Hadlee mould and it is worth noting that a major factor in their success has been the expert manipulation of that attack by Keith Fletcher.

BATTING

The captain clearly has a decisive role when his side is fielding, but it is not possible to influence matters to the same degree when the team is batting. Cricket has yet to reach the stage when the captain has a radio link with the two batsmen out in the middle so that he can issue desperate instructions such as 'Stop hooking. Your running between the wickets is diabolical. For heaven's sake hit him over the top.' It's probably just as well. Nonetheless, a captain can create a few ground rules to be adopted in the dressing room by the batting side.

Inverarity believes that 'it's no coincidence that successful sides sit together while the team is batting rather than wander everywhere; the players are involved in what is happening out in the middle'. This is still the case in Western Australia. When I played in Perth in 1986/7 I was

Keith Fletcher of Essex has been one of the shrewdest and most successful County captains of the last decade. He has quietly – and good humouredly – *tolerated some of the eccentricities of his own side, while remaining ruthlessly competitive towards his opponents on the field.*

struck by the contrast between that dressing room and Somerset's. During a County game at Taunton the lower order batsmen may take only a passing interest in the game's progress; the dressing room is often half full and the atmosphere is tranquil (especially since the departure of Ian Botham). In Perth, to my amazement and initial alarm, every scoring shot was enthusiastically applauded and my post-prandial naps constantly disturbed.

The captain may decide what is or is not acceptable during those hopefully long hours in the pavilion. In some dressing rooms the playing of cards is forbidden if play is in progress. On one England tour the management decided to ban players listening to personal stereos to prevent most of the side disappearing silently into a musical world of their own. Varying policies can be adopted, but it helps if the guidelines are clearly defined. Once I recall a captain having to remind his players to leave a few sandwiches for the incoming batsmen at tea-time.

Inverarity used to give his batsmen some sort of goal to

aim for, even if it was only 'you must be there at lunchtime'; he reckoned that batsmen play much better if they have specific objectives and he encouraged partners to set themselves targets while out in the middle. The captain's presence becomes crucial during a run chase; it is vital that he is on hand to deliver instructions to outgoing batsmen; he may say 'keep going for them' or 'block it up' or even the dreaded, ambiguous 'see how you go for a few overs and then make up your own mind'. This last instruction should only be issued to experienced players, if at all. Sometimes he may want to console a dismissed batsman and discuss what went wrong, though it is usually best to wait for a while. One former County captain was known to await the return of an outgoing batsman and to deliver a lengthy and vehement dressing down before the unfortunate had unbuckled his pads. This is not recommended.

The captain is responsible for deciding the batting order and some like to juggle with all sorts of permutations. In the Sixties one Somerset captain often instructed four or five players to pad up simultaneously to cover every eventuality. X would bat if the left-arm spinner was bowling, Y if it was the off spinner and the unfortunate Z got the hairy quicks. However, most batsmen prefer the stability of batting in the same place whenever possible so that they can develop their own routines. Inverarity recalls that Ross Edwards, one of his top players, capable of batting anywhere in the order, believed that he was most effective batting at No. 4. Since Edwards was so convinced of this, Inverarity decided that it was also in the best interests of the team that he should bat at No. 4 and prove his point. The captain cannot be so accommodating to every member of the side, however.

Inverarity once had an argument with Rod Marsh, who wished to bat higher than No. 7. 'I consciously prolonged the argument and in the end I yielded, since he was perfectly capable of batting higher. Marsh had gone out on a limb to get promoted so I knew that he would be very keen to prove himself right. Situations like that often arise and should be exploited if the player concerned has sufficient flair and talent.'

The Australian team crowds onto the balcony at Lord's as they stand on the brink of victory in the 2nd Test (1985). Whenever a side is batting well the balcony is invariably full; if it is in trouble, players tend to retreat inside and, if possible, watch the game on the television.

Sadly the skill of timing a declaration has declined, especially in club cricket where league systems have evolved which turn many games into a limited overs contest. Even in County cricket, the final innings is often viewed as an extended limited overs run chase. It is hard to generalize about what constitutes a good declaration, since many factors have to be taken into account. In *The Art of Captaincy* Brearley lists what he considers to be the most important ones:

'The relative strength of the captain's bowlers and their batsmen.

The time available.

The nature of the pitch.

The styles and attitudes of his bowlers.

The degree of risk that the competition and his team's standing in it permit.'

Obviously on pitches helpful to the bowlers the target can be less demanding and the captain should leave sufficient time to bowl the other team out rather than worry about run rates. At Leicester, Illingworth was acknowledged as an excellent judge of whether a wicket was suitable for a 'generous' declaration. On good batting surfaces a declaration may be the only way of producing a result, especially in three-day cricket. Here the target will be stiffer, but it is essential that it is sufficiently enticing for the batting side to try to achieve it, otherwise the likely outcome is the dullest of draws.

At Somerset in recent years, opposition captains have found it extremely difficult to know what is a realistic target because of the presence of Richards and Botham. Many have erred on the side of caution, since they have based their calculations on the assumption that one of them will hit a blistering century in an hour. Test matches rarely end in run chases created by a declaration; there is too much at stake. I think the last instance was in 1968 when Gary Sobers set England 215 in 165 minutes, a target they achieved. The press called it a 'sporting declaration', which the West Indian players probably regarded as a euphemism for 'a mistake by the captain'.

THE GUARDIAN OF ETIQUETTE

Ranji wrote in 1896: 'On his own ground a captain, as the highest executive officer, is, to a certain extent, in the position of host. He should see that the visiting side is

properly treated and their comfort consulted as far as possible. He should show a regard for them by welcoming them on their arrival and bidding them goodbye when they go.'

You may regard such an attitude as utterly outdated in the cut-throat modern world of professional cricket in the 1980s. I don't, and I'm pleased to report that even at the highest level most captains around the world still recognize that they have a role to perform as host. A couple of years ago Mark Nicholas was acutely embarassed by the standard of lunch during a County game and he offered profuse apologies to the Somerset team. At the end of play, County captains still ensure that their opponents are offered hospitality. In Australia, where cricket remains as competitive as it could be, the teams maintain the custom of gathering in one dressing room after play for a beer or two and a chat. It would be sad if these traditions died and at every level the captain is best placed to ensure that they are kept alive.

In the long run, maybe the captain's most important task is to be responsible for the conduct of his team. He should be severe on players who abuse batsmen, show dissent and question umpires' decisions. One of the most unlikely and, in retrospect, funniest sights I've witnessed took place in Lahore in 1984, and I hope Bob Taylor won't mind my

Left *Bob Taylor dismissed by Abdul Qadir in Karachi, 1984. It was during this series that Taylor was quietly reprimanded by Gower, much to everyone's amusement. A touring party can easily begin to feel isolated and victimized; often the players become over-sensitive about what they regard as bad umpiring decisions. The only solution, even though it can be a very difficult one to put into practice, is to accept the decisions and retain a cordial relationship with the umpires.*

Below *Even at Test level there is room for humour and friendly banter between opposing sides. Here Garner and Botham keep Lamb and Gomes amused; 3rd Test, Headingley, 1984. Significantly, England's captain in this match, David Gower, is too preoccupied by the state of the game to enjoy the joke. While being captain may be deemed a great honour and a privilege, the demands are equally great. In many respects, the captain's situation is not always an enviable one, as David Gower's expression suggests.*

recalling it. Taylor is justly regarded as one of the fairest and most gentlemanly players to have been in the game. In a Test against Pakistan he uncharacteristically showed dissent after the rejection of an appeal, so David Gower, England's captain, though 20 years Taylor's junior, took it upon himself to censure his venerable wicketkeeper for his lapse. Naturally Taylor accepted Gower's admonitions, which were hardly Dickensian in their ferocity, and the issue was quickly forgotten. Yet it was absolutely proper that Gower spoke to Taylor, even though the whole scene bordered on the absurd because of Taylor's previous impeccable record. It is vital that a captain should remember these responsibilities to safeguard the well-being of the game.

Finally, don't forget to thank the umpires at the end of each match; a good rapport between captains and umpires can diffuse an explosive situation swiftly. After the umpires, don't forget the groundsman, the tea ladies, the dressing room attendant . . .

As I said earlier, a captain's job is never done.

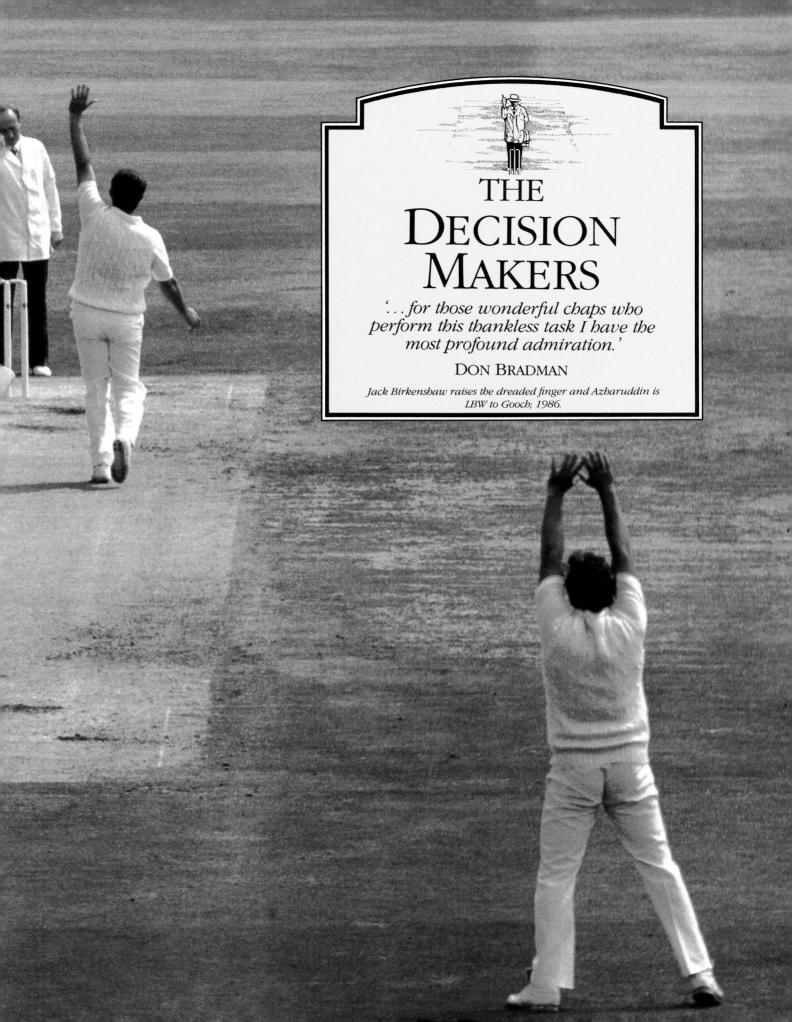

THE
DECISION
MAKERS

'...for those wonderful chaps who
perform this thankless task I have the
most profound admiration.'

DON BRADMAN

*Jack Birkenshaw raises the dreaded finger and Azharuddin is
LBW to Gooch; 1986.*

A good pair of umpires is as important to a cricket match as a sharp pair of scissors to a hairdresser. In *The Art of Cricket*, Don Bradman was quick to acknowledge their contribution – 'for those wonderful chaps who perform this thankless task I have the most profound admiration'. Yet there are times in every cricketer's career when he regards the umpire as something less than 'a wonderful chap'. Like politicians, their decisions rarely satisfy both parties; the batsman may be relieved, but the bowler disgruntled by the rejection of an LBW appeal (or vice versa). Umpires, like batsmen (and politicians again) cannot avoid making mistakes but the best, like Dickie Bird or David Shepherd, make fewer than most and they should command everyone's respect.

I talked to Jack Birkenshaw, not just because he has reached the top of the ladder as an umpire, but because his career reflects a life in cricket as a player, coach and umpire. Cricket has been his livelihood since joining the Yorkshire staff at the age of 18 in 1958. In the early Fifties he went to the same coach as Geoff Boycott – the diminutive former Somerset leg spinner, Johnny Lawrence. 'In cricketing terms I was brought up with "Boycs". As a 13-year-old he was no better than the others; he just practised harder and he hated losing his wicket even then. When he played in matches, he just stayed at the crease so he learnt to bat in the middle.'

Yorkshire had just superseded Surrey as England's premier County side and they had a superb bowling attack with Trueman, Wardle and Illingworth, their main match winners. Being an off spinner, Birkenshaw had few first team opportunities, and these were restricted to when Illingworth was on Test duty, so in 1961 he decided to join fellow Yorkshiremen Willie Watson and Dickie Bird at Leicester, where expectations were a little different. 'Leicestershire weren't used to winning; we accepted defeat easily and seemed to enjoy being beaten just as much as winning.' The arrival of Tony Lock as captain in 1964, however, coincided with an upsurge in Leicestershire's fortunes. 'Lock was still a great bowler and a superb catcher; his enthusiasm and enjoyment of the success of others helped improve our performances no end.' The revival was helped by the appearance of some sand on the Grace Road wickets so that the ball spun, and Lock and Birkenshaw both took more than 100 wickets per season.

Ironically, Lock was soon to be replaced as captain by Ray Illingworth, whose shadow Birkenshaw had already fled once. Jack stayed at Leicester, was successful enough to play for England five times in 1972/3 and remained generous in his assessment of his new captain.

'On a turning wicket he was magnificent: he bowled at a pace which was difficult to hit and he never gave a run away. He would take 7–20 rather than 5–50 if the ball was spinning. As a captain, like most Yorkshiremen, he was defensively minded, but once on top he would crush the opposition. If the wicket was helping the bowlers he would always leave plenty of time to dismiss the other side. Often we would go out to field with the opposition needing just 250 runs in a whole day to win, but Illy knew when the odds were stacked in our favour.'

While Illingworth wreaked havoc on turning pitches, Birkenshaw toiled uncomplainingly on the flat ones and in the nets as well, during the late Seventies when he became responsible for the indoor school at Leicester. As a coach, he monitored the progress of the young David Gower, but he didn't interfere much with such obvious natural talent. 'David always let the ball come on to the bat better than most, he stood still and he was a beautiful timer; you let players like that go their own way, while trying to make them realize how good it feels to score a century.' Brian Davison from Rhodesia was Leicestershire's other match-winning batsman in this era, and Birkenshaw's observations about him may be helpful to some. 'When Davison tried to defend he was hopeless. As soon as he lost his temper or decided to attack he was brilliant. When he was trying to smash the ball out of sight his feet were automatically in the right position; when defending they weren't.'

After a brief spell at Worcestershire Jack joined the umpires list in 1982 – with a little reluctance. 'I had hoped to get a coaching position, but the County coach is too often looked upon as a second-class citizen and there were not many opportunities.' It amazes me that County clubs have not attached far greater importance to the role of County coach in recent years. Very often he is poorly

Umpires, like cricketers, come in all shapes and sizes. On the right is Swaroop Kishan who has become an instantly recognizable figure in world cricket. Like Marilyn Monroe, he is splendidly photogenic. Umpires, too, fulfil several roles, one of which seems to be that of master of the players' wardrobe.

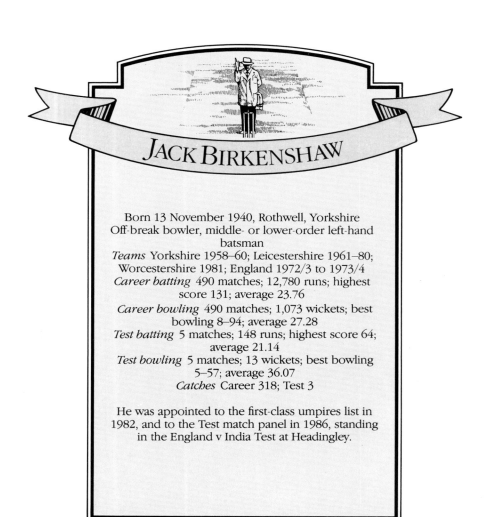

JACK BIRKENSHAW

Born 13 November 1940, Rothwell, Yorkshire
Off-break bowler, middle- or lower-order left-hand batsman
Teams Yorkshire 1958–60; Leicestershire 1961–80; Worcestershire 1981; England 1972/3 to 1973/4
Career batting 490 matches; 12,780 runs; highest score 131; average 23.76
Career bowling 490 matches; 1,073 wickets; best bowling 8–94; average 27.28
Test batting 5 matches; 148 runs; highest score 64; average 21.14
Test bowling 5 matches; 13 wickets; best bowling 5–57; average 36.07
Catches Career 318; Test 3

He was appointed to the first-class umpires list in 1982, and to the Test match panel in 1986, standing in the England v India Test at Headingley.

rewarded and has remarkably little authority when it would seem far more logical that, along with the captain, he should be one of the most influential men in the club.

So umpiring became the natural option for Birkenshaw. Umpires are now paid as much as the players and the job has maintained his involvement in the game, which he loves. The transition from player to umpire was not entirely smooth, however. 'I began thinking that I could still play the game and wishing that I still was. Bill Alley said to me, "Now you're an umpire, forget you ever played." He was right but it's hard to do that straight away.' There are obvious advantages, however, in being an ex-player.

'Since you know most of the players as friends, they usually want you to do well in the first couple of years. After that you stand or fall by your results. Also, you're so much more familiar with the game that, for example, you're more aware of the angles for LBW decisions; you've been studying them five days a week for the last twenty seasons. It is a unique situation in sport to have former players officiating and that's why there's often a special relationship between players and umpires. When I started as a youngster with

Yorkshire I remember how the old umpires would help, giving advice and encouragement; that was part and parcel of the game.'

Now Birkenshaw, who is a natural coach anyway, cannot resist doing the same and many young County pros have benefited as a result. Incidentally, the first class umpires list of 1986 contained just two names who have not played first class cricket.

Good umpiring often results from a happy partnership.

'If you've got a good mate at the other end, it's very enjoyable; if not, it's hard work. Six hours out in the middle is a long time and it's as important for umpires to help and encourage each other as it is for two batsmen involved in a long partnership. At the fall of every wicket I'll chat to my partner, reassuring him that all's going well or that there's just an hour to go.

Jack Birkenshaw has devoted his entire working life to cricket and he still enjoys it, whether playing, coaching or umpiring. County cricketers are fortunate that so many former players choose to go on to the umpires' list, and thus ensure that the decision makers are those with broad experience.

Tempers just occasionally become frayed at Test level. It is up to the umpires and captains to defuse the situation. Phil Edmonds is the object of the West Indians' displeasure.

This helps us both to relax and our concentration should improve as a result; sometimes I'll talk to the non striker or the square leg fieldsman in between balls if they're happy to do so.'

In English County cricket they usually are.

The ability to concentrate throughout the entire day is vital. Birkenshaw tells a story against himself: 'In my second year (1983), I umpired the NatWest Bank Trophy semi-final between Somerset and Middlesex at Lord's. It was a big game for me, with 20,000 spectators. By the last over the scores were level and Somerset needed either one run or to bat out the over to win the match. John Emburey bowled the final over to Ian Botham, who decided to block it out despite being on 96. On that day everything had gone brilliantly for me as an umpire until the last ball of the match. Emburey appealed but by this time I'd already picked up the stumps. My concentration had gone because the game was over (even if Botham had been dismissed, Somerset by virtue of losing fewer wickets would have won the match). The LBW appeal must have been close but I was in no position to give it. I was more concerned with getting off the field. Such a lapse of concentration could have been crucial in slightly different circumstances.' Standing upright for 6½ hours is hard enough; concentrating all the time throughout that period is even more demanding. Players should try to remember this.

The umpire's main function, apart from counting up to six, is to respond to appeals. Some may be raucous, aggressive shouts from a cluster of close fieldsmen, others polite inquiries from bowler and wicketkeeper; both deserve the same attention. I asked Birkenshaw what happens when he hears an appeal.

'Usually it is an instinctive reaction. With LBWs, for example, you might be certain straight away that it's out; but you have to pause for a while just to check that the batsman hasn't nicked the ball. But you shouldn't wait too long, since then a little glimmer of doubt is created. Normally your first, immediate impression is the right one. Once you delay, you're more likely to go wrong.'

The dismissals which require an umpire's decision are LBW, caught, stumped and run out. Birkenshaw observes, 'You have phases when your LBWs are good but the bat/pads worry you – just like a batsman having trouble with particular shots.' The laws are clear regarding catches, stumpings and run outs, even if they are hard to judge on occasions. The LBW law is more complicated:

'LBW
The striker shall be out LBW in the following circumstances:

a) *Striker attempting to play the ball.*
The striker shall be out LBW if he first intercepts with any part of his person, dress or equipment a fair ball, which would have hit the wicket, and which has not previously touched his bat or a hand holding the bat provided that:
   1) the ball pitched in a straight line between wicket and wicket or on the off side of the striker's wicket, or in the case of a ball intercepted full pitch would have pitched in a straight line between wicket and wicket;
   2) the point of impact is in a straight line between wicket and wicket, even if above the level of the bails.
b) *Striker making no attempt to play the ball.*
The striker shall be out LBW even if the ball is intercepted outside the line of the off stump if, in the opinion of the umpire, he has made no genuine attempt to play the ball with his bat but has intercepted the ball with some part of his person and if the circumstances set out in a) above apply.'

I hope that's clarified the situation.

In fact, most umpires find LBW one of the easiest decisions, maybe because they cannot be proved conclusively right or wrong by the action replay. For Birkenshaw there are a couple of 'regulation' LBWs – the shooter that 'nips back' into the batsman and the away swinger which started on leg stump and which the batsman has played across. Thereafter they become more difficult: plenty of balls that are going to hit the wicket hit the pad outside the line of the off stump and therefore 'not out' is the correct decision. Sometimes it is hard to detect whether a batsman is genuinely playing a shot when he thrusts out his left pad with his bat following in close proximity.

Below *Umpiring can be hazardous. Here, Roy Palmer ducks out of the way of a straight drive. I've seen umpires at the bowler's end retreat 6 or 7 yards when Botham is attacking the spinners.*

Right *A study in concentration. Swaroop peers over the bails as Underwood bowls. Swaroop's English is based mainly on his contact with touring sides – cheaper but less reliable than a language course.*

The umpire should also take into account from where the bowler is delivering the ball. If he is bowling from wide of the crease, the ball is less likely to pitch on the stumps as well as hit them. The bounce of the wicket is important: in Australia, umpires are particularly reluctant to give batsmen out on the front foot and this may well be justified by there being greater bounce from Australian pitches. For an ex-player on the umpires list these considerations may well be monitored automatically and taken on board but that is not necessarily the case with umpires who have less experience of the game.

Caught

Problems arise here with catches behind the wicket and in the bat/pad positions. Birkenshaw says,

> 'Few people walk nowadays. [To walk in cricket parlance is to give yourself out when you have snicked the ball to the wicketkeeper rather than waiting for the umpire's decision.] Umpires don't mind players standing, but they dislike players who walk one day and not the next, and especially those who put on a theatrical performance for the benefit of spectators and the media when they're given out.'

For catches behind, the umpire looks for the ball deviating after it has passed the bat and he listens for the sound of the nick on the edge of the bat. Often the most difficult to distinguish are down the leg side, since it can be hard to ascertain whether the ball has flicked the batsman's glove or thigh pad. Certainly the umpire should never allow himself to be swayed by the force of an appeal; his life would become a misery if he gained such a reputation. 'Even if you get three concerted appeals on the trot,' says Birkenshaw, 'you must keep saying "not out" until you know he's hit it.'

The number of bat/pad catches has increased significantly over the last 20 years, because the technique of batsmen facing spinners has changed. Johnny Lawrence would have taught the young Birkenshaw to play slightly in front of his pad so that edges tended to go behind the wicket. Now batsmen play behind their pad so that edges

Australia's Lance Cairns is caught by Allan Lamb at forward short-leg from Botham's bowling. The umpire, David Evans, must be certain of two things on this occasion. Did the ball carry? Did the ball cut the bat as well as the pad?

tend to pop up square of the wicket. In addition, the advent of helmets and shin pads has meant that fielders stand closer, so that more little nicks on to the pad reach them. Birkenshaw admits, 'From 22 yards it can be hard to be certain that the ball flicked the glove or the inside edge, but the golden rule applies – if there is any doubt the decision must be "not out".'

Stumped

Ranji, who probably didn't contemplate joining the umpires list, concluded that 'there is not much difficulty with stumpings unless the umpire has gone to sleep or is looking in an opposite direction'. There are a few points to remember, however.

The line belongs to the wicketkeeper, so that a batsman may be given out stumped if his foot is touching the line rather than positioned behind it. Also, the wicketkeeper can only take the ball in front of the wicket if it has touched the bat or the body of the batsman. Occasionally the ball can rebound from any part of the keeper's body on to the wicket; if the batsman is out of his ground this constitutes a stumping.

Run out

These occur more frequently now, notably at the end of limited overs matches. Birkenshaw explains the correct technique for the umpire at the bowler's end. 'You must get square of the wicket quickly. You should move the same way as the ball has been hit; you should be as far from the stumps as possible and perfectly still when the ball returns. However, if you follow this to the letter you can

Len Pascoe bowls a bouncer to Clive Lloyd; Adelaide, 1980. The umpire's outstretched arm indicates a 'no ball'. The umpire has also shouted his decision. However, the batsman has no time to adjust his shot against a fast bowler.

find yourself in trouble when the ball has been hit to mid-on. If you start to move to the leg side you can be right in the firing line if the mid-on fieldsman decides to throw to the wicketkeeper's end. It's better to be in the "wrong" position than in hospital suffering from concussion.' In one-day games the umpire has to be nimble and fleet-footed, which prompts Birkenshaw to observe that 'even umpiring has become a young man's job'.

The advent of the dreaded action replay machine means that clear evidence can be given these days as to whether the umpire's decision was correct when dealing with stumpings and run outs. Birkenshaw believes that umpires, especially since they are now better paid, should be prepared to accept some criticism, but with this proviso; 'Sometimes a batsman is shown to have been run out by three inches on the replay and the umpire has given him "not out". That's really an excellent decision, since in the heat of the moment there must be an element of doubt when the margin is so small. In those circumstances I think that commentators and journalists should heap credit rather than criticism upon the umpires.'

No balls, wides

Birkenshaw doesn't find these too much of a problem, though he acknowledges, 'The first time I ever called a no ball was nerve-racking because I suddenly had to shout and I was a little self-conscious. It can also be tricky when you have a bowler who is basically good (ie, his feet generally land in the same place well behind the line); you relax and then he can suddenly take you by surprise.' Most

The ubiquitous Swaroop finds the camera lens again. He is pointing out where the bowler's foot is landing. In County cricket umpires often informally warn the bowlers if they are 'getting close' to overstepping the popping crease. The bowler here is Winston Davis of the West Indies; Calcutta, 1983.

umpires in first class cricket let the bowler know if he's gradually 'creeping up' so that the bowler can make the necessary adjustment.

For those unfamiliar with the law regarding the position of the bowler's feet, here it is:

'LAW 24–3

'The umpire at the bowler's wicket shall call and signal "no-ball" if he is not satisfied that in the delivery stride;
a) the bowler's back foot has landed within and not touching the return crease or its forward extension; or
b) some part of the front foot whether grounded or raised was behind the popping crease.'

Remember that a batsman can only be dismissed off a no-ball by being run out and that the bowler must bowl an extra delivery to complete the over.

What constitutes a 'wide' depends on whether it is a first class or limited overs match. In first class cricket the ball has to be out of reach of the batsman, but the interpretation in limited overs cricket is much stricter in order to prevent negative bowling down the leg side. In one-day games different umpires' interpretations often vary considerably. That doesn't matter too much, though it is important that the same umpire should be absolutely consistent throughout both the innings. It is relatively easy to call a wide in the middle of the first innings, but it takes a good deal more mettle on the umpire's part to do so at the end of the second when the outcome of the match is in the balance.

A batsman may be out hit wicket, stumped or run out from a wide delivery – but not bowled.

Signals

The hand signals performed by the umpire during the course of a match are not designed simply to be part of the entertainment to keep the spectators amused: they constitute his method of communicating with the scorers. It is important that the scorers and umpires should have a good rapport. Before the match the umpires should ensure that they know the whereabouts of the scorers on

Dickie Bird doing his Norman Wisdom impression. Dickie's mannerisms have become part of the English game, yet they are totally natural and unforced.

Players always look forward to matches in which Dickie is standing. First, he's an excellent umpire, and second he's good company.

the ground and that they are both in position and ready when the game starts. For their part, the scorers should swiftly acknowledge the umpire's signals so that the game can proceed without delay.

These are the signals:

Boundary 4:	by waving the arm from side to side.
Boundary 6:	by raising both hands above the head.
Bye:	by raising an open hand above the head.
Dead ball:	by crossing and recrossing the wrists below the waist.
Leg bye:	by touching a raised knee with the hand.
No ball:	by extending one arm horizontally.
Out:	by raising the finger above the head.
Short run:	by bending the arm upwards and by touching the nearer shoulder with the tips of the fingers.
Wide:	by extending both arms horizontally.

Jack Birkenshaw believes that the role of the umpire has become steadily more demanding over the last 20 years. Today's umpires must be capable of operating mechanical aids such as light meters and pocket calculators; their decisions are under closer scrutiny than ever before via television; players no longer 'walk' and are more desperate for success at any cost; umpires now often have to stand their ground against concerted appeals from almost the entire fielding side. Occasionally a game may start to fray at the edges, in which case it is the umpire's responsibility to calm everyone down again – usually with a quiet word to the bowler or captain.

Despite all this, Birkenshaw still loves his involvement with the game and regards the player/umpire relationship in County cricket as being a very healthy one. I agree with him and I would recommend that all players note the words of Ranji on this subject.

'There is much that is difficult, monotonous and thankless in an umpire's task. So perhaps it will not be out of place to remind all those who take part in the game to avoid showing disgust at umpires' decisions. I am afraid umpires sometimes meet with unkind and even abusive language. Never abuse an umpire. You may meet him again and he is hardly likely to be prejudiced in your favour if you talk to him as if he were a pickpocket when he has given you out.'

Even a prince can be pragmatic.

POSTSCRIPT

Concerned lest the more innocent among you were actually tempted to accept the author's rather ungenerous assessment of his cricketing skills, we thought it both wise and fair to provide a sober corrective in the form of a career profile. You may judge for yourselves, but we hope you'll be agreeably surprised to learn of his achievements and be reassured that you were in very capable hands.

MARKS, Victor

Born 25 June 1955, Middle Chinnock, Somerset
All-rounder – off spin bowler – middle-order right-hand batsman
Teams Oxford Univ 1975–8; Somerset 1975–;
Western Australia 1986/7; England 1982–83/4
Career batting 266 matches; 9,873 runs; highest score 134; average 30.10; 112 catches
Career bowling 266 matches; 636 wickets; best 8–17; average 33.04
Test batting 6 matches; 249 runs: highest score 83; average 27.66; no catches
Test bowling 6 matches; 11 wickets; best 3–78; average 44.00

His Test matches have been in England, New Zealand and Pakistan, and he has also toured Australia. His stand of 167 with David Gower at Karachi in 1983–4 is England's best for the seventh wicket against Pakistan. He has played in 33 limited overs matches for England, scoring 285 runs (highest 44), average 13.57, and taking 44 wickets (best 5–20), average 24.45, with 8 catches. He represented Oxford University at rugby fives.

Below and right *Vic Marks playing for Somerset.*

INDEX

Tom Spencer's verdict . . . ?

ACKNOWLEDGEMENTS

We are especially grateful to Keith Andrew and the National Cricket Association for their generous assistance throughout the project and for placing at our disposal the coaching skills of Bob Carter, Doug Ferguson and Graham Saville as well as a fine array of cricketing talent in the form of Mark Ramprakash, Michael Atherton, Michael Cottam and Peter Rochford, who were patient and exemplary models for the artwork references; and to Kim Deshayes and Tim Crow of the TCCB for being our editorial safety net.

Thanks are extended to the following for allowing us to quote from material which is their copyright: Hodder & Stoughton Limited and David Higham Associates Limited for the extracts from Donald Bradman's book *The Art of Cricket*; Hodder & Stoughton for the extracts from Mike Brearley's book *The Art of Captaincy*; William Collins for the extract from Dennis Lillee's book *The Art of Fast Bowling*; and the MCC for the extracts from the rules of cricket.

Finally, we wish to acknowledge the following as the sources of the photographs: All-Sport 14, 101, 176, (Adrian Murrell) 46 above & below, 48, 76, 83, 109, 111, 113, 117, 128, 131, 132/3, 141, 154, 155, 159, 161, 167, 169; Camera Press 149; Colorsport 1, 9, 49, 57 above, 61 below, 114–5, 122, 135 above; Patrick Eager 2/3, 10/11, 13, 17–25, 28/9, 31–43, 45, 50–4, 57 below, 59 above & below, 61 above, 63–75, 79, 84–100, 103, 104/5, 108/9, 110, 112–3, 114, 118/9, 123–7, 129, 135 below, 137, 138, 143–53, 156/7, 162/3, 164/5, 166; National Westminster Bank PR 7; Photo Source 44; Bob Thomas 170, 171.